D0841720

Buddha Heart Parenting

Buddha
Heart Parenting

❧

Enrich your family with
Buddhist wisdom and compassion

❧

CL Claridge PhD

Vajra Publications
Kathmandu, Nepal

Published by
Vajra Publications
Kathmandu, Nepal

Distributors
Vajra Book Shop
Jyatha, Thamel
P.O. Box: 21779, Kathmandu, Nepal
Tel.: +977-1-4220562, 4246536 Tel./Fax: +977-1-4220562
e-mail: bidur_la@mos.com.np
www.vajrabooks.com.np

Front cover photo by Caesar Ursic
Back cover photo by Rodolfo Clix

ISBN 978-99946-788-39

Printed in Nepal

May all sentient beings
achieve enlightenment

Acknowledgements

This book would never have been written if it were not for my children. They inspired in me a passion to 'get it right' and to do the best I could for them. When they were born I became committed, not only to them, but to all children and their parents. Children are the future and if we can enable them to reach their Buddha potential, we have achieved something worthwhile.

My children are very dear to me. They each have their own place in my heart and I thank them deeply for being in my life and for their contribution to the writing of this book.

I would also like to thank my daughter-in-law, Shannon, whose clear insights added warmth and value to an early draft.

To the thousands of parents I have worked with over the years I would like to express my sincere appreciation. You helped me to refine the skills and knowledge that are described in this book. As you learned so did I. We travelled the path together.

As a practicing Buddhist I am on the bottom rung of the ladder in my understanding of Buddhist philosophy. My very sincere gratitude goes to Venerable Tenzin Chönyi (Dr Diana Taylor) for her invaluable advice and support. She meticulously read and edited the draft manuscript, not once but twice. Many times she questioned my interpretation of Buddhist principles. For this I am most grateful. Not only because I can now be confident the book is accurate in its Buddhist detail, but also because by questioning my interpretation she caused me to reflect more deeply on details of Buddhism I thought I understood but actually had misunderstood.

Working in many countries, my Buddhist study largely has been centred on books and on teachings that coincided with my whereabouts. Without Geshe Tashi Tsering at Chenrezig Institute and Lama Zöpa Rinpoche for inspiration my study would have lacked a certain dimension of humanness.

A book about parenting is a book about family, and I would not be the person I am today if it were not for my parents and brother. As with all families they have played an integral role in my life. My parents helped shape my early years. My brother, Gordon, prepared my eyes for Buddhist philosophy. Thank you.

Finally, there is my life partner – who could wish for anything more. Words of thanks could never be enough.

Contents

Foreword

Being a parent is hard work. My own father once said to me, whatever you do it is wrong. I was a teenager at the time, so his comment was not surprising, but whatever mistakes he thought he had made, he must have done something right. These days we siblings get on well. He and my mother had laid the basis for this early in our childhood. Not that they were perfect either. They both frustrated and fulfilled me. Any book which helps parents negotiate the minefield of bringing up children is welcome.

There are many books about child-rearing, but few which base it firmly on Buddhist principles. Buddhism, in the end, is about cause and effect. If we do something positive it will have a positive effect. It is an optimistic philosophy in which it is possible to achieve complete elimination of all ignorance and therefore of all suffering. We may not be able to do this in one short lifetime, but we can make a start. For this reason, the teachings of Shakyamuni Buddha begin with where we are now. His methods for dealing with life were not just for monastics, but also for the householder, the parent. These teachings and methods are the wisdom wing of Buddhism

The other wing of the Buddhist bird is that of compassion. What does it mean to be compassionate to a child in a temper tantrum, or wheedling for the latest toy? What does it mean to be compassionate to an 18 month toddler compared with a 6 year old in Grade 1? Parents these days are challenged in a way that they have never been challenged before. Our children live in a society which pushes them to want more and more and yet is alarmingly polluting the world in the process.

Although the context has changed, the ways in which we interact with each other, for good or ill have not changed over 2,500 years. We are still caught unawares in patterns of anger, disappointment, overreaction and wanting so much for our children to be happy that we are in danger of creating the opposite effect. The value of this book is that it combines Buddhist practice with CL Claridge's years of working with children, including her own. I am delighted that her commonsense and kindness have found expression in this book.

Venerable Tenzin Chönyi (Dr Diana Taylor)
Touring Teacher, FPMT
(Foundation for the Preservation of Mahayana Tradition)

Why Buddha Heart Parenting?

A family is a place where minds come in contact with one another. If these minds love one another the home will be as beautiful as a flower garden. But if these minds get out of harmony with one another it is like a storm that plays havoc with the garden.

Buddha

In this section the author discusses why Buddha Heart Parenting is the most effective and appropriate parenting approach to use. Here we will find explanations of why parents need Buddhism and why Buddhists need parenting. This provides the background understanding for the integration of Buddhist philosophy with contemporary psychology to form Buddha Heart Parenting.

- **The Opportunity Presented to Parents**

- **Why Parents Need Buddhism and Why Buddhists Need Parenting**

The Opportunity
Presented To Parents

In what is seen, there should be just the seen;
In what is heard, there should be just the heard;
In what is sensed, there should be just the sensed;
In what is thought, there should be just the thought.

Whether you are a Buddhist with an interest in parenting or a parent with an interest in Buddhism, this book will show you how to create a powerful

> Engaged Buddhism is a term coined in Vietnam by Thich Nhat Hanh emphasising action based on awareness.

synergy from the two and become an effective and compassionate parent and an *engaged Buddhist*.

We can all benefit by using the principle of action based on awareness and driven by compassion and wisdom. What parenthood provides us is an extra motivation and opportunity for inner development and greater understanding of Buddhist principles than we find in other aspects of our life.

Practicing Buddhism whilst parenting children is, in principle, no different from practicing Buddhism without parenting children, we are still working with our mind. But we have a fortunate life indeed if we share it with children. Children provide us with a myriad of opportunities to deepen our practice and to fully engage in the practice of Buddhism. They allow us a precious opportunity to **practice** and **live** the Dharma.

Those who see worldly life as an obstacle to Dharma see no Dharma in everyday actions; they have not yet discovered that there are no everyday actions outside Dharma.
                    Thirteenth Century Zen Master Dogen

Many people think that the best way to practice the Dharma is in a meditation cave. Few of us can live ascetic lives in isolated places, but we can all practice the Dharma in the here and now, no matter where we are and no matter what our life situation. Buddhism emphasises a personal responsibility for inner development through a rational, deep and sophisticated approach to human life.

This is why personal responsibility for inner development, i.e. development of the mind, is emphasised in parenting from a Buddhist perspective. This approach uses a combination of skills and strategies, together with compassion and wisdom, to achieve success – success in parenting and success in our inner development. I call this approach to parenting Buddha Heart Parenting.

I developed Buddha Heart Parenting™ to provide parents, grandparents and caregivers with an ethical approach to parenting and child-raising that is based on the Buddhist principles of compassion and wisdom. This approach to parenting is simple, easy to follow and use, and results in connected relationships and self-empowered children. I coined the term, Buddha Heart Parenting, because when we parent using Buddhist philosophy and principles we are operating from our Buddha heart or *Buddha nature*. We are parenting as if we are Buddha.

> 'Buddha heart' or 'Buddha nature' is the potential of our mind to become the mind of a Buddha. We have always had this potential, and always will.

When we understand that all *sentient beings* have the same innate nature that wants happiness and doesn't want to suffer, we are more easily able to maintain compassion and loving-kindness. This innate nature is the drive within all of us to become 'better' people, because by becoming 'better' people we gain some measure of happiness. Even though we sometimes 'mess up', all of us are doing the best we can at any given time – our children as well.

> Sentience is the quality or state of being sentient – consciousness. It is the capacity for basic consciousness or the ability to feel or perceive.

We all have a tendency to focus on ourselves. We tend to think that other people and our children 'make' us feel angry, hurt etc through their behaviour. Buddha Heart Parenting gives us skills to look at the underlying causes of our children's behaviour, and realise their behaviour is driven by how they feel. We can take this realisation into our meditation and look towards all other people, and realise that their behaviour is also a reflection of their state of suffering or happiness. This realisation helps us to remain calm in the midst of personal conflict, and to respond with compassion and wisdom.

When we strive to understand why people behave how they do, the focus is taken from ourself and put on others. From looking firstly at the causes of our children's behaviour and the behaviour of members of our immediate family, we can then look at our wider family. What we see is that behind all *unskilful* or inappropriate action lies

> Skilful when used in its Buddhist context combines the technical sense of the word present in its use in the English language with the moral sense of the Pali *kusala*. Thus skilful action has both a technical and moral element. Skilful action is motivated by compassion. Unskilful action is generated through ignorance and/or an intent to harm.

suffering – these people also suffer and want happiness. We can then feel heart-warming love for our wider family. Next we can turn to our society and then to the world and bring this understanding of suffering causing unskilful action to everyone, and so develop heart-warming love to all.

From this heart-warming love comes compassion, that is, a desire for others to be free of suffering and its causes. Our meditation on understanding others and developing compassion has been successful when we feel for all unhappy beings the way a mother feels for her only child when that child is sick. Whatever the mother is doing – eating, walking, etc – she has her child in her mind, feels his or her suffering is unbearable, and wishes her child to be free from it. These are the feelings we take into our meditation on compassion. Parents, therefore, have a unique opportunity to develop compassion.

By developing universal compassion we can quickly grasp the understanding that our children are suffering if their behaviour is inappropriate. In this way, we can remain calm and to choose a response that will be most helpful in that situation. Otherwise we are prone to react and cause further suffering for the child, and for ourselves.

There are many other useful Buddhist techniques that are valuable in helping us develop compassion for our child, and stay calm in the midst of the turmoil of parenthood. Three of these are particularly useful and easy to use. One is the realisation that during the aeons of lifetimes we have experienced, our child would have been our mother at some time. Knowing that they have suffered for us helps us to maintain our equilibrium in the face of provocation. Another practice is to realise that our child could be a Buddha who has chosen a rebirth that will help us to reach enlightenment. Lastly, we can focus on the Buddha potential that resides within our child.

These techniques are extremely useful to practice, not just once but many times – especially when we are feeling angry with our child. It can be useful to remember that without the difficult situations that are often part of parenthood we would not have the opportunity to practice the Buddha's teachings. Without the grit the pearl will not develop.

The aim of this book is to enable us to be Buddhas, to awaken the Buddha within us and let that guide all that we do in our parenting role - that is, to engage in Buddha Heart Parenting. This will result in relationships with our children based on compassion. Our children will also develop compassion. When we use Buddha Heart Parenting our children will have a greater ability to reach their potential and achieve true and lasting happiness.

The focus of this book is on the 'how'. How do we parent through a Buddha heart? Early chapters of the book discuss why we act as we do in our parenting role, and why children behave how they do. With this understanding and the skills and tools outlined in later chapters we will be able to transform our relationships with our children and transform our life. Emphasis is placed on the Buddha's core teachings of compassion, impermanence, emptiness, and dependent origination and on how to integrate these concepts and qualities into all aspects of parenting by following the Eightfold path and the guiding paramitas or practices of generosity, patience, meditation, morality, energy and wisdom.

This book shows why some of the current approaches to parenting are often ineffective and why they don't fit with Buddhist philosophy. This book also shows how some of the popular tools for parenting can do more harm than good. There are other contemporary theories of child psychology and behaviour change that can work hand in hand with Buddhist psychology, and we will see how these theories compliment one another and provide a powerful tool for transformation.

Will Buddha Heart Parenting work? It has for me and for many others. Just as the Buddha asks us to listen and reflect and not to take teachings without questioning, so when reading this book take time to reflect on the accuracy or truth of the material for you. Put into practice and judge for yourself. Maybe you just want to hone a few skills, but still you want your parenting to be better, better for you and better for your children.

I firmly believe that all parents want a relationship with their children based on compassion and peaceful coexistence. Too frequently the advice we are given for dealing with our children falls short of really helping to achieve this. Behaviour management techniques that focus on reward and punishment are not the answer, as they do not support our child to develop their Buddha heart. There are some parenting techniques that are effective in changing external behaviour, but without the underlying Buddhist motivation and attitude they fall short of answering our need for parenting techniques that advance our child and ourselves on our spiritual path, and that give us relationships based on compassion and peaceful coexistence. What we need is a middle-way approach in which family relationships are transformed to be based on compassion, wisdom and peace. This is possible for each of us if we apply ourselves to such a transformation.

How to use the book

The transformation we seek may take time and effort. We will need to work on our inner development while at the same time developing our skills and parenting practice. We can develop a program of meditation and study of Buddhist principles and concepts that allows us to devote at least a few minutes a day to this inner development. This book is written to enhance and support this study and inner development, whilst providing practical skills to help put our Buddhist understanding into practice with our children.

When you read about the different skills and strategies and how they follow Buddhist principles and concepts, you are sure to experience an 'Ah, that is so true' feeling. What I have written connects deeply within us all to our compassionate Buddha heart. It is from our Buddha heart that we can operate in all aspects of our life not just in our parenting role.

So I suggest you read the entire book once to gain an understanding of the underlying motivation and ethos, and an understanding of the 'big picture' of Buddha Heart Parenting. Then go back and choose skills you wish to develop. It is up to you to decide the order in which you would like to acquire these skills. I suggest starting with easy ones. Work on developing one skill at a time. When you feel you have mastered a skill, move on to the next.

The skills and strategies need to be practiced and it can take time to change any of our current inappropriate responses

> Samsara refers to the constant cycle of birth, suffering, death, and rebirth.

to our children's behaviour. These responses have become habituated over time and we need time to habituate new, appropriate, skilful responses.

Be kind to yourself. Recognise that your development may not be linear. You may progress quite well and then relapse into old habits. This is normal. Have compassion for yourself. Don't beat yourself up. If you have started to read this book then you are moving in the right direction. Your Buddha heart cannot be denied.

Wealth and possessions chain us to samsara – parenting can help to set us free.

Why Parents Need Buddhism and Why Buddhists Need Parenting

If what you are doing, isn't working, stop doing it and do something different.
Definition of clinical insanity is to do something over and over again that is not working or not beneficial.

Compassion and wisdom lie at the heart of Buddhist philosophy. This combination of compassion and wisdom is just as essential to parenting as it is to Buddhism as a whole. They form the two wings of the bird – without one, the bird cannot fly. In parenting, compassion without wisdom, leads us nowhere. We need wisdom to know how to apply compassion. Compassion without wisdom can do more harm than good to our children and to our relationship with them.

The Buddhist teacher Chogyam Trungpa Rinpoche used to distinguish between 'compassion' and what he called 'idiot compassion'. Idiot compassion is compassion without wisdom. This is a very apt term, because when we use idiot compassion we may feel 'good' because we think we are helping our child, but we are acting like an idiot or a foolish person who is oblivious to reality and the real impact of our actions.

For example, we may feel compassion for our child when she is devastated by something one of her friends said to her and we may think we need to interfere and 'fix' it up. But in so doing we may prevent our child from learning from the experience.

Another example: Our young child is always demanding sweets and lollies. He continually cries and pleads with us to give them to him. Out of compassion, we give them to him. When he is older, his teeth have numerous cavities, he is overweight, and he is unhealthy.

In these two examples if we had combined compassion with wisdom we would have acted very differently and our actions would have been beneficial to our child. Only with wisdom can we know how to respond when we feel compassion.

When we combine compassion and wisdom to parent through our Buddha heart we impact not just our lives and the lives of our children. As parents we are in a unique position to affect people on a wider scale. Buddha Heart Parenting can lead to internal transformation that leads to world peace – world peace can only come about through the development of inner peace in the individual.

Peace is not external, it is internal and *mindfulness* together with equanimity helps create inner peace. Many people think that if they meditate they will gain peace. This is true to an extent but meditation takes place not just on the meditation mat. Meditation occurs when we are being mindful in the moment in our daily life. Take the example of washing dishes – we can mindfully wash dishes to get them clean or we can mindfully wash dishes to wash dishes. That is, we can concentrate on the experience of washing dishes. If we decide to be mindful of washing dishes then as Thich Nhat Hanh says – the purpose of washing dishes is not to get them clean - the purpose of washing dishes, in this case, is to wash dishes. We can be mindful of the purpose we choose while at the same time being mindful of the activity.

When we play with our children, we can decide what to concentrate on. That is, we can decide what to be mindful of. We can play with them to teach them skills or to keep them quiet, or we can play with them to have joy and delight in the interaction and the action. Either way we can be mindfully in the moment. Similarly, we can choose to read to our children to simply read and experience joy and delight in the interaction, or we can choose to help them learn how to read or to increase their knowledge. In our communication with our children we can choose to mindfully communicate.

> Mindfulness is a state of awareness of the object we want to concentrate on. The experience of mindfulness is one of clear alertness. The word 'mindfulness' comes from the Pali word 'sati' which is an activity. So mindfulness is something we do.

We choose what we are going to be mindful of and having made that decision, we are not mindful of other things. We have this choice. We can use this opportunity with wisdom and compassion to decide what we are going to be mindful of in our children at this moment, and in a few moments later.

Mindfulness brings inner peace and by being mindful we will be spreading peace in every moment. When we are peaceful, calm, and filled with loving-kindness our children will internalise these attributes. And our children will feel valued. They may also learn new skills or they may behave appropriately during and after our playtime. These are secondary benefits.

Peace is available to us if we can quiet our distracted mind and be in the moment. When we achieve this, we feel happy and we smile. Just as our smile lights our face, so too does our smile light our child's heart. A smile relaxes our facial muscles, nourishes awareness and calms us miraculously. This sense of calm supports us in our parenting.

As we develop the qualities of compassion and bodhichitta or altruism within ourselves we are then able to create an atmosphere of peace and harmony, firstly in our family, then our community and ultimately in the world. This is why in our meditation we can focus on compassion and on

> Bodhichitta is defined as the wish to achieve total enlightenment for the sake of all living beings. Bodhichitta holds two thoughts, (1) wanting to be a Buddha in order to (2) fulfil the desire to help all sentient beings.

developing a motivation to reach enlightenment to benefit all living beings, that is, *bodhichitta*.

With bodhichitta you become so precious – like gold, like diamonds.
You become the most perfect object in the world, beyond compare with any material thing.

Lama Yeshe

If we can create this atmosphere in our family and help our children to develop inner peace through developing compassion and altruism the impact we have for peace can become exponential.

The Buddhist path supports us in developing altruism or bodhichitta. It leads us away from the self. Buddhism shows us how we can use every situation that comes our way to develop our Buddha heart and bodhichitta.

Whilst some readers may be familiar with Buddhist philosophy and the Mahayana tradition, others may not. The overview below is brief but sufficient to an elementary understanding. We will all benefit from continuing to study and practice Buddhism. There are a few resources that may be useful, listed at the end of the book.

In general terms, Buddhism is a way of experiencing the world – it is common sense. It is often almost impossible to get in touch with common sense because of our *ignorance*.

Ignorance is a state of mind that does not correspond to reality. Ignorance creates suffering by obscuring the fact that things are impermanent and/or interdependent

Common sense is lucidity about what is a reasonable and beneficial way to live. When we strip away the attachments, aversions, greed, egoism etc that result from ignorance we are left with Buddha nature or Buddha heart. I prefer to use the term Buddha heart because it emphasises the 'heart-felt' aspect of Buddha nature.

The Buddha taught a method of how to live life from our Buddha heart, and in so doing provides us with an accurate psychological explanation of the actual nature of *mind*. Psychology literally means a study of the mind, and much of Buddhism reads like cognitive behavioural therapy.

Who was the Buddha we hear so much about? He was the great teacher referred to as Gautama Buddha or Shakyamuni Buddha. Over 2500 years ago Shakyamuni Buddha was born as Siddhartha Gautama, a prince. Sheltered from real life for the early part of his life he began to question the meaning of life when he eventually did see aging, sickness and death. He subsequently renounced his prestigious position and the privileged life he was born into, and set upon a search for answers. For six years he became a wanderer seeking the teachings of the leading holy men of his time. During this time he followed firstly, the teachings of indulgence and then of asceticism, but neither gave him the answers and wisdom he sought. After a serious health crisis Siddhartha decided to sit beneath a pipal tree (now called the Bodhi tree) and meditate until he either found the wisdom he sought or died. Fortunately for all of us he attained enlightenment. He found the answers he sought. He was then called the Buddha or Enlightened One.

Through the pleading of his disciples Sakyamuni Buddha realised that what he had learnt would be of use to others. He then set about teaching others what he had learned. He continued to teach constantly until he died at just over eighty years of age. He gave his first teachings on the basic understanding of Buddhism - the Four Noble Truths. It is these four noble truths, along with the Eightfold path, (the fourth noble truth), that are the most basic and important Buddhist beliefs.

> Mind is defined in Buddhism as a non-physical phenomenon that perceived, thinks, recognises, experiences and reacts to the environment. The mind is described as having two main aspects: (1) *clarity*; meaning that the mind is clear, formless and allows for objects to arise in it, and (2) *knowing*; meaning that the mind has an awareness, a consciousness, that can engage with objects.

The First Noble Truth is the truth of dukkha. Dukkha is often translated as suffering but a more correct translation is dissatisfaction. Dukkha embraces all types of unpleasurable experiences and can range from mild dissatisfaction to great suffering and pain. Dukkha includes pain, sorrow, frustration, anger, remorse, repulsion, agitation, and depression. This suffering can be broken into three different types:

- **Manifest Suffering** – these are the more obvious sufferings of loss, pain, illness, and mental and emotional disharmony.
- **Suffering of Change** – short-lived happiness. Inevitably whatever gives us perceived happiness in the physical world does not last.
- **Suffering of Conditioning** – conditioning of the mind, i.e. karma that is perpetuated from one life to the next.

The Second Noble Truth is the origin of suffering. The truth is that suffering has a cause. There are two types of causes:

> Delusion is belief in something that contradicts reality. It is a lack of awareness of the true nature of things, or of the true meaning of existence. We are deluded by our senses, among which intellect is included as a sixth sense.

- Actions contaminated by *delusions*, which create the imprints, or karma; and
- Delusions themselves – these include attachment/aversion, anger, desire and our fundamental ignorance.

The Third Noble Truth is the cessation of suffering. Suffering can cease. Even the suffering of parenting can cease.

The Fourth Noble Truth explains the path leading to that cessation. This path is the Gradual Path to Enlightenment, or Lam Rim teachings, and contains an extensive explanation of the Eightfold path, which is a lesson plan in wisdom, ethics and meditative skill. In order to follow this path we are advised to cultivate eight aspects:

1. **Right View or Right Understanding.** Right view means to see and to understand things as they really are.
2. **Right Intention.** Right intention can be described as commitment to ethical and mental self-improvement.
3. **Right Speech.** Right speech means to refrain from pointless and harmful talk.
4. **Right Action or Conduct.** This aspect relates to the body as a natural means of expression and refers to deeds that involve bodily actions – including speech.
5. **Right Livelihood.** Right livelihood means earning one's living in a way that is not harmful to others.
6. **Right Effort.** Right effort means to direct our efforts continually to overcome ignorance.
7. **Right Mindfulness.** This refers to the ever watchful, attentive mind, and being aware of what we are attentive to.
8. **Right Meditation or Contemplation.** Right meditation is earnest thought on the deep mysteries of life.

We will look at the Eightfold path in much more detail later as it is forms the basis of Buddha Heart Parenting. If we develop and operate from these eight aspects we are actualising our Buddha heart.

The Eightfold path is one way of explaining the last of the four noble truths. These four truths and their understanding provide a basis for successful practice of Buddhism. Without proper insight into the first two truths and their interrelationship, no genuine aspiration to seek freedom from cyclic existence can arise. Without insight into the last two and their interrelationship, no genuine release from cyclic existence can be achieved.

The four noble truths are set within a Buddhist context of the mind. The mind, in Buddhism, is not located in the brain, but in the heart. So, parenting through a Buddha heart is parenting through a Buddha mind. The mind refers to all conscious and unconscious aspects of ourselves. It contains imprints that affect the conscious mind. It is the part of us that conceptualises, experiences, perceives, feels and thinks.

One of our aims in studying Buddhist teachings is to transform our mind and heart. The body and mind are two different continuums. The body has form, the mind is formless but is nevertheless a phenomena. The mind is conscious and life occurs when the body and mind are interrelated and death occurs when the two continua are separated. At death the body simply disintegrates, whereas the mind takes another rebirth determined by our actions or karma in this life and previous lives.

Each individual's stream of consciousness (subtle mind), has, since beginningless time, been polluted by ignorance, *attachment*, and *aversion*. The influence of these negative thoughts causes us to create further negative karmic seeds to reside in our stream of consciousness or mindstream, the result of which is the experience of suffering, such as rebirth in unfortunate states, pain, illness and all the other misfortunes of emotional, financial, and physical health that befall us and others. Despite these negative thoughts always having been there, they are not a permanent part of the mind and they can be completely eradicated. When eradicated, the mind's basic clear light nature is revealed and suffering ceases.

> Attachment is the exaggerated not wanting to be separated from someone or something. Aversion is the opposite of attachment. Aversion is the exaggerated wanting to be separated from someone or something.

Nothing can come into being without a cause. There is no independent arising. Past actions and thoughts create habits, patterns and karmic seeds that influence our current life, and our current actions and thoughts influence future lives or our future in this current life.

Mahayana Buddhism. Although this book applies Buddhism to parenting or parenting to Buddhism in a way that is relevant to all schools of Buddhism, the underlying approach I take is of Mahayana Buddhism. The Mahayana Buddhist tradition is believed to have been founded by Nagarjuna sometime in the period 100BCE – 500CE. Mahayana Buddhism is referred to as the Middle Way and establishes a framework for the teachings of emptiness and the path of the Bodhisattva (someone who has entered the path and is deeply motivated to attain enlightenment in order to benefit others most effectively). The practitioner of Mahayana emphasises altruism and has as her primary motivation the liberation of all others, for which she needs her own freedom from cyclic existence. All Buddhist practitioners emphasise the presence and possibility of Buddhahood for us all, believing that the seed of Buddhahood (Buddha heart) lies within each creature and that there is no fundamental difference between the Buddha and anyone else.

This is Buddhism in a nutshell. We need to study and develop our Buddha heart. Learning the skills of Buddha Heart Parenting without furthering our understanding and practice of Buddhism will not achieve the results we want. In later Chapters we look at impermanence, compassion, emptiness and dependent origination and the Principle of Cause and Effect as they relate to parenting.

Understanding Behaviour

True Essence

The essence of true mind
Transcends causality and pervades time.
It is neither profane nor sacred;
It has no oppositions.
Like space itself, it is omnipresent,
Its subtle substance is stable
And utterly peaceful;
Beyond all conceptual elaboration.
It is unoriginated, imperishable,
Neither existent nor non-existent.
It is unmoving, unstirring,
Profoundly still and eternal....
Neither coming nor going,
It pervades all time,
It permeates all space...
All activities at all times are manifestations
Of the subtle function of true mind.

Chinul, Korean Ch'an Master
(1158-1210)

From the background understanding of why Buddha Heart Parenting is the most appropriate parenting approach to use, this section goes on to give an explanation of why we parent how we do and why children behave how they do. This helps us to understand how the different parenting styles affect children, and how children's behaviour is an expression of their needs, either met or unmet..

• **Why Do We Parent How We Do?**

• **Why Do Children Behave How They Do?**

Why Do We Parent How We Do?

We are what we think.
All that we are, arises with our thoughts.
With our thoughts, we make our world.

Buddha

Different Parenting Styles

Why do we parent how we do? Maybe we can understand ourselves as parents if we check out the different ways that we

> Parenting style describes the way that parents attempt to control and socialise their children.

parent. There are five basic parenting styles – **authoritarian, permissive, guilt-swing, democratic or authoritative,** and **Buddha Heart.** Most of us have a predominant style that we use most of the time, although we may use other styles on occasion.

The different parenting styles suit different socio-political contexts and this is clearly illustrated when we look at Western societies.

The Authoritarian Parent

Most parents prior to the 1950s were authoritarian and set clear, and often unbending, rules for what a child could do and could not do. Misbehaviour was strictly punished. This parenting style was mirrored in the school system where students did not question the teacher and were punished for misbehaviour. Authoritarian parenting often produces rebellion, and produces children and adults who will unquestioningly follow others (not just appropriate role models). Children of authoritarian parents tend to be anxious and withdrawn, to have low frustration levels for difficult tasks, to do well in school and be well behaved socially, at least while authority figures are present. Times have changed and it is easy to see that parenting in this way is at odds with a socio-political situation that values choice and innovation.

The Permissive Parent

The permissive parenting style was popular in the 1950s and 1960s after the negative examples of dictators in World War II became well known. It is a swing away from the political system. Parents may choose this laissez-faire method of parenting as a reaction to having grown up with strict, authoritarian parents and so decide not to discipline their children.

Another reason parents may choose this permissive style is because they are under a lot of stress and do not have the energy to make rules and enforce them. Children are allowed free reign and are encouraged to think for themselves and to value non-conformity. They are encouraged to express any and all emotions with no guidance or limits on behaviour. However giving children free reign does not always support them in reaching their potential and in developing compassion, loving-kindness and the skills of cooperation and collaboration. For example, without intervention, a bully stays a bully because this kind of behaviour is an effective way to have needs met. These children are sowing negative karmic seeds and the result will be suffering. Where there is a bully there is also a more passive child. Bullies seldom pick on someone who can stand up to them. Without intervention, the passive child, the victim, may continue through life as a victim because this is how they come to see themselves.

Children of permissive parents tend to have difficulty regulating their emotion, to be defiant when desires are challenged, to have little staying power for challenging tasks and tend to engage in antisocial behaviours.

In the 1950s and 1960s it was almost always the case that one parent was consistently available to guide the self-discovery of the consequences of actions. Therefore the child had one person who was on the lookout for dangerous and more harmful consequences of their child's uninhibited behaviour. Whereas today, most families have both parents working even if one is only part time, and the child is under the care of several adults, or at times under the care of none. In this situation the permissive parenting style is even less appropriate.

The Democratic Parent

As a result of the mismatch of both the authoritarian and permissive parenting styles with our current socio-political situation many parents have adopted a democratic (sometimes also called authoritative) parenting style. Democratic parenting focuses on children learning to take responsibility. Parents set realistic guidelines for children and use a range of techniques to ensure they are met. The techniques parents us include rewards, praise, and punishment (usually not harsh punishment). Communication is a focus of this parenting style. Children of democratic parents tend to be well adjusted, to have confidence in themselves, and have appropriate social skills.

The Guilt-Swing Parent

Other parents feel guilt for any of a number of situations they control, for example, guilt over not spending enough time with their children, guilt about not having enough money to give children what they think their children should have, maybe guilt about a marriage breakdown, guilt about how they parent, guilt about being too overweight to play with their children, guilt because they are striving to build their career and are spending little time with their children. This guilt for perceived deficiencies creates parents who feel they need to make 'it' up to their children and so swing from too little parenting to too much parenting. The too-little parenting happens because of their fast lifestyle, their race up the career ladder, their two working parent families, or one parent families where that parent is working. The too-much parenting happens because they feel guilty and want to make reparation and they do this by parenting too much, by catering to their child's every whim, doing school projects for or with them and being 100 percent in their face. But this cannot last for long because of the reasons they have for too-little parenting, so the parents feel guilty. Hence the guilt-swing is in full motion.

The Dismissive Parent and the Disapproving Parent

Other parenting styles that you are sure to recognise are the Dismissive style and the Disapproving style. These styles are variations on the previously described basic styles.

The **dismissive parent** is uncomfortable with their child's negative emotions. They tend to say things like:

> *"Stop crying and get over it."*
> *"You don't have a problem. You're just being too sensitive."*
> *"It's all right. Everything will be fine."*

Dismissive parents say these things either because they don't know what else to say or because they think the child's feelings are unimportant. Some parents always 'fix' their children's problems. They have ready solutions and are more than willing to share them. For example:

> *"Oh, you dropped your ice-cream. Don't worry, I'll buy you another."*

These parents fall into the category of dismissive parents too. One of the major problems with dismissing a child's feelings is we are teaching them that there is something 'wrong' with having negative feelings and that we 'shouldn't' have them. This discourages a child from bringing these feelings to their parent.

The **disapproving parent** disapproves of, or punishes, a child for having negative feelings such as sadness or anger. Typical comments are:

"If you don't stop crying, I'll give you something to cry about."
"Stop being angry with him. It's not nice!"

This style of parenting also tells our child there is something 'wrong' with negative feelings, and because it tries to force our child to stop the feelings it can lead to emotional difficulties later. Children who experience these comments often have difficulty regulating their own emotions and solving problems and have lower self-esteem.

The Buddha Heart Parent

The parenting style that is timeless and appropriate for all historic periods is one based on the Buddhist teachings and especially on compassion, loving kindness and cooperation – Buddha Heart Parenting. Buddha Heart Parenting is a step beyond democratic parenting. It builds on the communication skills of democratic parenting to create compassionate communication. Where democratic parenting uses punishment, rewards and praise, Buddha Heart Parenting instead uses techniques that focus on enabling our child to know they are in control of their lives, and supporting them to develop their Buddha heart. Parenting through our own Buddha heart makes the difference. By treating our children as equals in human worth and dignity, we base our relationship with our children on mutual respect and compassion.

Our role is more as an enabler, as a facilitator of our children's empowerment. We guide our children and oversee their wellbeing. Our goal is their empowerment, to instil self discipline, not to reward and punish our child in order to control her or to teach her appropriate behaviour. The system of reward and punishment is counter productive to what we are ultimately trying to achieve.

Ultimately our child is the master of her own destiny. Our role is to help her develop the skills and knowledge that allow her to achieve this effectively. We need to treat our children how we would like to be treated. As adults, do we want to be told what to do or not do, be punished and rewarded, not listened to, not be part of decision-making that affects us?

How do we choose our parenting style?

Why do we parent how we do? Where do these styles come from? For most of us, we subconsciously choose our parenting style based on the way our parents parented and on the socio-political context in which we live. We learn many skills and ways of doing things from our parents in our early years through the process of socialisation. How many of us have found ourselves saying something and then thinking 'that sounded just like my mother/father'? Sometimes the style of parenting adopted by our parents affects our choice inversely, that is, we may parent differently than our parents did simply because we didn't like the way they did it.

Some of us consciously choose our parenting style. We attend classes or read books because we want to do what is 'right' for our children. In doing this it is important that we do not just unthinkingly take on someone else's ideas, but reflect on them. It will often be clear when we read something if it is 'right' for us. When this happens we think it makes perfect sense and we resonate with the ideas expressed. We feel comfortable with the suggested parenting techniques.

But to make sure we are not just reinforcing an inappropriate or ineffective parenting style from our parents or from our patterned existence, we need to understand why the parenting style is appropriate and effective. In Buddhist terms we need to understand why it is skilful action, and how it fits in the Buddhist path for ourselves and for our children. We need to understand how it can further our children's spiritual growth and help to advance them on their spiritual path.

For most of us our style of parenting is habituated by the time our child is approximately 3 years of age. This doesn't mean that we can't change but we have to realise that behavioural patterns have been set up and these may take time and effort to change. Changing a behavioural pattern is more difficult than creating one, but with knowledge of why we parent how we do and why our children behave inappropriately, along with new skills and techniques, all of us can learn to parent through our Buddha heart.

Our parenting style can also be the expression of patterns and karmic imprints. The mind is a pattern-making organ – the more we do something or think something the stronger the pattern. That is, the more familiar we are in behaving or thinking in a certain way, the stronger will be our tendency to act that way again. If we have a habit of thinking in a particular pattern, positive or negative, then these tendencies will be triggered and provoked very easily and recur and go on recurring. Most of us habitually indulge in anger and attachment, but not in virtuous thought, joy, loving kindness, and generosity.

It all arises in the mind. We create our experiences and conditions by our thoughts. All the apparent positivity and good times in our lives are a result of cause and *condition*. Similarly all the negativity and troubles in our lives are a result of cause and condition. They are not in our true nature nor do they occur by chance. The conditions we find ourselves in today are a result of our thoughts and actions in the past. This is good news because it gives us hope.

> **Condition.** Conditions are the secondary causes, e.g. the sunlight is a condition for the ripening of a seed, but the main cause for the seed to ripen is the potential inside the seed for growth.
> The cause for karma ripening is an imprint on the mind made by past thought and behaviour. The conditions for karma to ripen are the external circumstances that trigger that imprinted cause into a result.

We can do something to have the kind of future we want. Our future conditions will be a result of our thoughts and actions today. It is how we respond to the circumstances we find ourselves in today that will determine our future circumstances.

> *"Our life is shaped by our mind; we become what we think. Suffering follows an evil thought as the wheels of a cart follow the oxen that draw it.*
> *Our life is shaped by our mind; we become what we think. Joy follows a pure thought like a shadow that never leaves."*
>
> The Dhammapada

How our children's behaviour impacts on us emotionally and mentally is a result of our past. But we can control how things impact us emotionally and mentally and so we can take control of, not only our present, but our future as well. We have the ability to control our destiny, including the state of our body and mind. By the model we provide, we influence our children to sow positive or beneficial karmic seeds, which can ripen in their future. Each one of us has unlimited potential. All we have to do is develop that potential.

How can we change?

How can we control how we feel when our children behave inappropriately? There are many ways. If we have a better understanding of why our children behave the way they do, that is, of what needs of theirs are unmet or met, then we will be better able to respond skilfully. Similarly if we have a better understanding of the reasons why we feel and respond the way we do (i.e. what needs of ours are met or unmet), we are less likely to think and act unskilfully. The absence of clear understanding is the basis for every negative feeling emotion we have.

This chapter has provided an understanding of why we parent how we do, while the next chapter helps us to understand why our children behave how they do. Other chapters help us to apply Buddhist principles to developing our Buddha heart and then to operate through our Buddha heart to parent our children.

When we practice mindfulness and *'looking deeply'*, we will very quickly recognise our own feelings and emotions in response to our child's behaviour and we can find ways to transform these feelings and emotions. For example, we have the opportunity before the feeling overtakes us to ask ourselves 'Why do I feel this way? What has happened?' What has happened is usually a threat to our pride, or self-concept, or possessions etc. We feel we need to maintain our ego, image, attachments, or we feel we need to have control, respect etc. But these needs are not real. They are figments of our imagination. These kinds of 'needs' are called perceived needs.

> To **look deeply** means to look into our mind beyond superficial thoughts. The result can lead to insight into the true nature of reality. We see our inner mind.

If we see things for what they are, none of this will bother us. We thought our happiness was threatened, but our image, attachments etc, can only give us temporary happiness. Lasting happiness cannot be affected by anything external to our mind.

Why Do Children Behave How They Do?

Easily seen are others' faults,
Hard indeed to see are one's own.
Like chaff one winnows others' faults,
But one's own (faults) one hides,
As a crafty fowler conceals himself by camouflage.
Dhammapada – Malavagga-Impurity, Verse 252.

We have just looked at what we do in our parenting role, and we saw that there is a complex mix of forming agents and reasons. There also is a complex mix of forming agents and reasons for why children behave how they do.

Having a good understanding of why children behave inappropriately assists us in developing ways of helping children to change. When our child is behaving inappropriately, and we are at our wits end, rather than loosing our cool we can stop and reflect on what our child must be feeling to act that way. Clearly they are suffering. If they were happy, their behaviour would reflect this. They would be cooperative and express loving-kindness to all those around them. Remember what it feels like when everything is going well and we feel loved – we feel centred and we have more patience, tolerance, and love than at other times. Loving our child as we do, we don't want them to suffer, instead we want them to have happiness and its causes.

If we find out why our child behaves in a certain way, we can more easily remove some of our emotion from the

situation and see more clearly what our child's needs are and
how we can best help and support them.

Appropriate vs. inappropriate behaviour

Children's behaviour can be categorised as either appropriate
(for the circumstances or for the child's age) or inappropriate
(for the circumstances or for the child's age). Children's
behaviour is often said to be 'good' or 'bad', or it is said that
children misbehave, or that they are 'naughty' or that they are
'good' boys or girls. I believe there is no such thing as 'good'
behaviour or 'bad' behaviour, neither are children 'naughty' or
'good', and I believe 'misbehaviour' is an inappropriate label.

According to the dictionary 'misbehaviour' means bad
behaviour or wrong behaviour, and children's behaviour is
neither of these things. Since circumstances are always
changing Buddhists do not tend to say that actions, by
themselves, are right or wrong. They may be right or wrong in
terms of advancing us along our spiritual path, but the actions
alone are not right or wrong. Children's behaviour is only
appropriate or inappropriate, or in Buddhist terms skilful or
unskilful, or beneficial or non-beneficial. Looked at in this way,
the child's, behaviour can be seen to be clearly separate from
the child's intrinsic Buddha heart. We need to develop the
clarity and insight to see things as they really are - to be aware
of our clouds of delusion. Behaviour is just that – behaviour.
Separating the behaviour from the child helps us to respond
with compassion and wisdom.

What determines children's behaviour?

Why do children behave appropriately and inappropriately?
Just as our behaviour is determined by our needs, either met or
unmet, so is our children's behaviour determined by their
needs, met or unmet. They have physical needs and
psychological needs. Our role as parents is to meet those needs

or to support our children so they can meet those needs themselves.

From my experience the major psychological needs of a child are:

1. Recognition and Inclusion
2. Autonomy and Influence
3. Cooperation and Contribution.

Children have a number of other psychological needs, which are discussed in later chapters, but the six needs listed here are the ones that determine most behaviour. When these needs are unmet children's behaviour is usually inappropriate, and when they are met their behaviour is appropriate.

For many of us, these same needs drive our own behaviour. As we, and our children, move along the spiritual path and realise the true nature of reality and our own Buddha heart, these needs diminish and so too does our inappropriate and unskilful behaviour.

Children have a need for recognition and inclusion

The most common unmet need that results in inappropriate behaviour is the need for recognition and inclusion. Children need to have recognition, and acknowledgement that they exist. They need to feel significant. Infants will literally wither and die without human contact. They need physical touching and verbal communication. In other words they need acknowledgement that they exist and that they have some significance. Within the family context, the vast majority of children receive sufficient recognition and acknowledgement and are given sufficient significance to ensure they survive but many times the only way (or the main way) they can get this acknowledgment is by behaving inappropriately.

Inappropriate behaviour gets recognition. Children need recognition and any kind of recognition will do. If they can't get positive recognition then negative recognition is better than no recognition at all. That is, if children do not get recognition in a positive way with love, cuddles, positive communication etc, they will try to get it in a negative way with smacks, shouting, name calling, punishment, etc. This may seem strange to us but if we realise that their very survival depends on getting recognition of some kind, we can understand why children would resort to triggering this negative kind of acknowledgement if they are not receiving sufficient positive recognition. Their significance needs to be acknowledged. They need to know they belong in the family and that they are loved and secure, and that they are valued.

Children have different ways of seeking recognition. Children will try out many different kinds of behaviour in their attempts to be recognised and feel significant. They will eventually settle on those behaviours that 'work' i.e. those that the parent or caregiver responds to. In other words they will keep trying new behaviours till they find our 'buttons', and then they will push these buttons until we respond. We all have different buttons and children may use different behaviours with different adults to get the response they want.

Some children become 'parent deaf' as a way to gain recognition and acknowledgement. These children have learnt that their parent has a 'don't ignore me' button, and when ignored the parent will go on and on and on.

For example, Stuart would tell his son to do something, and his son would ignore him. Dad thought his son hadn't heard him and so would repeat his instruction over and over again. He reasoned that until he got an answer from his child, the child must not have heard or understood what he said. Each time dad repeated what he said he would become more and more annoyed and insistent. You could see the child thought it was a great 'game' and would often smile as he ignored his dad. Before long dad would end up shouting and threatening the child with punishment if he didn't do what he was asked. This child has very successfully learnt how to make his father give him time and attention.

It is important to remember that children and teenagers are often not consciously aware of their psychological needs. It is also important to realise that when children have their needs met, their behaviour is appropriate. We can help them to entrench these behaviours with feedback and other skills described in later chapters.

The first thing to do in helping our child to change inappropriate behaviour is to try to understand 'their unmet need'. If this is not clear to us we can use empathic listening, which is one of the compassionate communication skills also described later in the book.

In the 25 years I have been teaching parenting education one of the most important things I have found is that behaviour is a result of met or unmet needs and that we can help our child by having their needs met. When parents are first introduced to this idea, they say it is too simplistic. They say the strategies cannot work so easily. But a couple of weeks later they will all be reporting that it *is* that simple and the strategies *are* working miraculously. If there is one understanding that can dramatically transform children's behaviour and build sound parent/child relationships this is it. **Our behaviour and our children's behaviour is determined by needs, either met or unmet!** Sure other understandings and strategies are needed but this one is the base from which to build.

Guidelines for giving recognition and inclusion

When our child is behaving inappropriately and we identify that she is seeking or demanding recognition we need to do two things – one at the time our child is behaving inappropriately, and one at other times. **Firstly, and most importantly, we need to give our child recognition when she is not demanding it.** We need to recognise that children need attention and that if they are given quality attention and recognition they are not likely to behave inappropriately to get it.

Giving children attention is a little like filling a bucket. If the bucket has a hole in it, it will never be filled – if the child demands attention, it creates a hole in the bucket and the attention falls straight through the bucket out the hole. We can never fill the bucket. Another way of looking at it is, when the child is demanding attention inappropriately they are holding their bucket upside down, that is, the wrong way up. They are going about having their need met the 'wrong' way. Attention we give them when their bucket is upside down doesn't go in the bucket.

We know what it is like when we ask our partner: Do you love me? They answer "yes", but we wonder if they said that because we asked, or because they feel it. Notice the difference when they spontaneously say they love us. We don't doubt it and we feel really loved. This is the same when children demand attention and then get it – the attention has little value.

Secondly, in the moment that our child is inappropriately trying to gain recognition, we need to ignore the behaviour. One of the best ways to extinguish inappropriate behaviour is to ignore it. But we need to be consistent. If we ignore an inappropriate behaviour for 30 minutes but then give in, our child has learnt that she may have to continue the behaviour for 30 minutes but **we will** respond eventually.

Don't ignore a dangerous activity. If there is any safety risk to our child or anyone else then we need to take action to ensure everyone is safe. This applies no matter what strategy we are using. We can ensure safety without giving the child the recognition they are trying to get. For example, if the child is hurting another child to get our attention we can remove the other child without giving any recognition to our child in the process, or it may be enough to remove a potential weapon from her hands. Always ensure safety.

We need to be aware that children can use seemingly 'positive' or appropriate behaviour to demand recognition and attention. For example, they can ask 'why' questions *ad infinitum*, not listening or taking any notice of the answers.

These children are not interested in the answers we give, so it is clear they are not asking questions to get the answers. These children may be seeking attention inappropriately. If we give these children more quality time and recognition when they are not demanding it, the incessant 'whys' may disappear. 'Why' will mostly be used when they want some information or explanation.

Another example may be a child that tattletales in a way that makes it look like she is just keeping the parent updated on what is happening. Or it may be a child who is a goody two-shoes and who is being in-your-face good. We have all come across this kind of behaviour. The child will be **too** helpful, **too** polite, **too** smug in her tattletales, **too** grown up for her age, and often **too** cute. Some parents would not see her behaviour as inappropriate, but she has found that she can only belong and have significance if she is super 'good'. This robs her of feeling loved for her own intrinsic self. She feels that to be loved and lovable she has to get recognition and attention by pleasing. Therefore this behaviour is inappropriate.

Our children need to feel included. They need to feel they belong. When we identify this as an unmet need in our child, we need to take extra time to include them in decision-making. Perhaps they can help decide what to make for dinner, or, when shopping, they can help decide which brand of food to buy. When we talk with our child as we would with a friend, he or she feels inclusion. Another way to build inclusion is to structure family meals so that everyone eats and communicates together (without TV).

Children need autonomy and influence

All children strive for autonomy, independence and for a feeling that they can influence the things around them. In Western cultures autonomy and independence may be a double-edged sword. Our culture probably has gone too far with individuation and independence of the individual, and we need to help our children to understand the *inter*dependent nature of all things.

Our children seem to have an inbuilt drive to learn skills so they can look after themselves. They need to have some physical independence. The tantrums of a two year old are a result of their need for independence being thwarted. And many power struggles we might have with our child are a result of their need for independence and autonomy being unmet. Contributing to these struggles can be our *perceived need* for control or influence. We may not feel our need for autonomy and influence is met.

> Perceived needs are false needs we think we have that are based on our attachments. For example, we might think we have a need for a clean house, but we actually have an attachment to having a clean house and an aversion to a dirty house. The need appears real because of our state of *ignorance*. Similarly, we may think we have a need for control, but as we study Buddhist teachings and put them into practice this need will disappear.

If our child is trying to get us into a power struggle there are again two things we need to do – one when they are behaving inappropriately and the second, at some later time, when their behaviour is appropriate.

Firstly, as soon as we realise there is a power struggle about to happen or is happening, we can withdraw. **Secondly,** and most importantly, we need to realise that if our child is having power struggles with us, they need more power over their own lives i.e. they need more independence and autonomy.

If we recognise there is a power struggle happening, or one is likely to start, we can withdraw. Withdraw from the struggle – disengage from the battleground. It is impossible to have a power struggle with someone who is not having one with you. This does not mean that our child will immediately abandon their attempts to win. They are used to us responding in a certain way and they may keep going to try to provoke us. When we withdraw we may have to withdraw from the scene as well as withdrawing from the interaction. We may need to remove ourselves to some other part of the house or if the battle follows us, we may retreat to the toilet and close the door.

Sometimes it is difficult to withdraw from a power struggle because we have been in it just as much as our child. Power and winning can be important to us too, because our needs for autonomy and influence may not be met. But if we realise that the withdrawal from conflict is only a temporary measure until the child's inappropriate power bids are extinguished, then we find it easier to withdraw. It can be agony for a parent to walk away from a power struggle and know that the child will continue to do what we have demanded they stop (or will do what we have told them they cannot do). But it is the only way to build the relationship and show our child that power struggles are not appropriate.

Remember if there is a risk of physical harm, take action, but we need to make sure we are not increasing the power struggle in the process. For example, Tom was working on his computer and his two sons were playing nearby. Tom's older son became very noisy and Tom found it very distracting. Tom demanded he stop making so much noise. He didn't stop, in fact, he became even louder. Tom became more demanding and ordering. Then he realised a power struggle was happening. He decided to withdraw and not insist they stop playing so noisily. In an attempt to get Tom back into the power struggle, his son started to hit his younger brother with a sharp toy. The younger child was at risk of physical harm, so Tom picked him up and took him to another room. Because he did this without talking and in a calm manner his older son didn't intensify the power struggle.

As I mentioned earlier, **we need to realise that if our child is into power struggles they need more power over their own lives** i.e. they need more independence and autonomy. We can let them have more control over aspects of their daily life that are appropriate for their age. For example, we can create situations where 4-6 year olds can make decisions about what clothes to wear, what to eat, what to take to school for lunch, where to sit at the table. This doesn't mean the child can decide to wear dirty play clothes to school or that they will eat lollies for dinner. But they can make decisions within acceptable boundaries.

The important thing is that the child has choices. The choices show the boundaries. We might put several sets of clothes in different drawers for different occasions. A 'school' drawer, an 'outside play' drawer, a 'going out' drawer, and the child chooses from within the appropriate drawer. We might provide a list of the acceptable foods for school lunches and the child chooses what they want each day. Etc etc. For an older child they can have a role in deciding what amount of TV they watch per week and which programs (within guidelines), or what time to come home after school, or which friend to invite on a family outing, or where the family goes for holidays. Etc, etc. With these choices our child will have many of his psychological needs met. He will feel significant and have the acknowledgement and sense of belonging he needs, as well as having satisfied his need for autonomy and independence. He will therefore have little reason to engage in inappropriate behaviours to get these needs met.

When we allow our child greater autonomy and independence by sharing decision-making with them they come to feel that they have influence. When parents use compassionate communication and talk respectfully to their children the children feel their ideas and opinions are valued and this increases their sense of having influence.

Children have a need for cooperation and contribution

Children need to have opportunities to cooperate and contribute. In many families the parents do all the housework and cooking themselves. They think it is too messy to have the children help, or they may think that childhood is a time for playing, and that there will be time enough for them to have to work. These are misguided perceptions. If children feel they are part of the family they will want to share the tasks around the house. It fills their needs for cooperation and contribution. One of the best ways children can learn to cooperate is by learning from the model their parents present. If we cooperate with children and their needs they will naturally want to do the same with us. This is especially the case when they feel they are our equals – in human worth and dignity. Teaching our children household tasks when they are young equips them with skills and attitudes that benefit them throughout their life.

When we adopt Buddha Heart Parenting methods our child will blossom. Their self-concept and self-confidence increases and when this happens they want to cooperate and make a contribution to the family. Children will feel responsible and be confident making decisions. They will develop compassion for others and be able to withdraw from conflict and power struggles out of a desire for peaceful resolution.

Why is it important to recognise needs?

Understanding that our behaviour and our children's behaviour is determined by needs, either met or unmet is a powerful realisation. When we see that behaviour is a result of feelings, and feelings are a result of met or unmet needs, we are able to see our children's inappropriate behaviour objectively. This allows us to easily separate the behaviour from our child and to have compassion and to respond with wisdom.

External influences on behaviour

Met and unmet needs are the main reason why children behave how they do, but there are other reasons as well. Children are bombarded with messages, information, and influences from many sources. Parents are only one influence on children's development, with peers, school and the media playing an increasingly large role. Children's behaviour and how they view themselves are also affected by their psychological position in the family constellation.

Influence of role models

When children are young they are most influenced by parents and adult extended family members. Children are most likely to model the behaviours of the parent or caregiver who is most warm and kind and who the child likes the most. Modelling is an important way for children to learn appropriate behaviour.

> *Modelling isn't the best way to teach – it is the only way to teach.*
> Albert Schweitzer. (attributed to)

The corollary of this is: What ever is modelled is taught – even if unintended. As parents we need to be aware that it is not just our 'good' behaviour that our children will adopt. They will adopt any behaviour we have.

Young children will also copy the behaviour of their siblings and friends, but usually to a lesser extent than they copy parents. Whether these modelled behaviours continue or are extinguished, is largely due to how parents respond. As children grow older their role models become the members of their peer group and older role models such as pop stars. Their peer group is not only children they associate with directly but also children they see and identify with on TV or in movies. The adult influence (parents, teachers, other family members) becomes less important. This is one reason why it is often more challenging to parent an adolescent. And a reason why it is useful to establish a social group with an interest in Buddhism and in parenting using Buddhist philosophy.

Influence of the wider environment

Television and the wider environment outside the family have a considerable influence on our children and how they behave and develop. Thich Nhat Hanh in *Peace in Every Step* says:

> *"Television sows seeds of violence and anxiety in our children, and pollutes their consciousness, just as we destroy our environment by chemicals, tree-cutting and polluting the water. We need to protect the ecology of the mind, or this kind of violence and recklessness will continue to spill over into many other areas of life."*

Corporate advertisers are having an increasing influence on our children's values, beliefs, wants, and behaviours. In many cases these advertisers have wedged themselves into the space between parents and their children. They employ the best psychologists and market researchers to lure children to products and values we, as parents, often don't approve of. With the advent of the electronic media, parents are finding it increasingly difficult to shield their children from the negative influence of the media. The morphing of advertising into life extends to schools as well.

How the family dynamic can influence behaviour

Children find a role for themselves through trial and error. The role they choose is influenced by; the family atmosphere and values, their role models, parenting style, and the psychological position in the family. This process starts early in childhood but is decided as early as 4-6 years of age.

The most significant trigger may be competition between siblings, which results in one child excelling in one area while the other chooses another area or skill. A child is usually influenced most strongly by the sibling who is most different from themselves, because intense competition with that sibling influences personality formation. It may be the competition between the siblings makes one child believe she has to be the best all the time. But it can also be a result of the family's beliefs. Some families may instil a belief that 'You can't trust anybody", or 'If somebody picks on you fight back'. In this way children develop their approach to life.

Once a child has decided a role, they will often stick to it even when they are adult and the role is no longer appropriate. The role may be as the 'clown' of the family, or the 'baby' of the family, or the 'good' boy, or the one who excels academically, etc.

When we value each child for their intrinsic Buddha heart, recognise the special attributes that each child has, and use compassion and wisdom in our interactions with them, negative influences from outside the family will play a lesser role.

What is 'inappropriate behaviour'?

Having talked about behaviour stemming from met and unmet needs it is time to look at just what is inappropriate behaviour. After all, what is seen as appropriate for some parents is inappropriate for others. Even within individual parents ideas about what is appropriate behaviour and what is not tends to change with experience,

> Dharma refers to the body of teachings expounded by the Buddha. It also refers to the principles or laws that order the universe.

maturity, and our knowledge of the *Dharma*. As we develop and overcome our ignorance we see things more clearly, we see things for what they are.

There are two ways of looking at 'appropriate behaviour' – appropriate for the age of the child and appropriate for the situation. Many parents complain of their child's inappropriate behaviour but the behaviour is in fact age appropriate. If an eighteen month old child draws on the walls it would not necessarily be intentional inappropriate behaviour. It might just be that there was a wall and crayons and the child felt like drawing. Whereas if a seven year old were to draw on the walls it is likely to be intentional inappropriate behaviour, and the child could be attempting to meet a psychological need.

A behaviour is inappropriate for the situation when it is performed in a place that is not appropriate. For example, kicking a soccer ball in the park is appropriate for the place, whereas kicking it in the lounge room is not.

Just as children's behaviour needs to be age appropriate so too does our parenting need to be appropriate for the age of the child. It is detrimental to children to either baby them or to expect them to act older than their years. Our behaviour towards our children needs to be respectful and age appropriate.

For example, most children go through a time of not wanting as much physical affection as they have had, or of wanting it in a different way. The physical expression of our love for our children needs to change over time. Obviously, it is not appropriate for a mother to cuddle a teenage son and smother him with kisses all over his body as we would if he were an infant or toddler. Children are often the first to signal it is time to change the way we express our love for them. If we continue to smother our child with kisses despite his or her struggles, thinking 'they really like it' or that it is good for them, they will feel disrespected. What they are learning is that if you are bigger than somebody, you can force yourself on them physically even if the other person is saying 'NO'. None of us want to be passing this attitude to our children especially not to our sons.

Another example, some parents expect their young children to sit quietly for long periods of time while the parents work or talk to other adults. This is expecting too much of young children. If children are provided activities or games at these times they are able to play quietly and not disturb their parents for a longer period of time.

Our perception of behaviour may be distorted

Many times we see, or notice, only inappropriate behaviour despite this being only a small part of the total behaviour of our child. This may be a result of attentional bias. Our mind uses attentional bias when it allows us to see things we wouldn't have seen before. I remember when I was pregnant I saw many pregnant women in the shopping centre. They seemed to be everywhere. Yet the number had not increased. I was just using attentional bias. When you buy a new car in a certain shade of colour that you think will be different, you quickly start to notice all the other cars the same colour. Before you bought the car your attentional bias didn't let you see the other cars that colour.

When looking at our children we often focus only on behaviour we find aversive. This is an attentional bias. Mindfulness is also an attentional bias. We can choose what we will be mindful of. We can choose to focus on our child's appropriate behaviour. This act of mindfulness will result in their appropriate behaviour increasing and their inappropriate behaviour decreasing.

Venerable Tenzin Chönyi says we are in charge of where we look, whether we look backwards at the inappropriate behaviour or forwards to a new beginning. Both views are valid. The important thing is to understand we have made the choice of what we are focusing on.

From my verandah

From my verandah I can look
up the valley
or down the valley
but not both at once.
When I contemplate the past
I can choose to see with anger
or contentment,
but not both at once.
I can choose to remember failure
or achievement,
but not both at once.

It does not matter whether I look
up or down the valley,
but it is important to know
which way I turn my eyes,
that I have chosen to do so,
and that I see only half the view.

Venerable Tenzin Chönyi (Dr Diana Taylor)
(reprinted with permission)

Building a Strong Base for Buddha Heart Parenting

Know all things to be like this:
A mirage, a cloud castle,
A dream, an apparition,
Without essence, but with qualities that can be seen.

Know all things to be like this:
As the moon in a bright sky,
In some clear lake reflected,
Though to that lake the moon has never moved.

Know all things to be like this:
As an echo that derives
From music, sounds, and weeping,
Yet in that echo is no melody.

Know all things to be like this:
As a magician makes illusions
Of horses, oxen, carts and other things,
Nothing is as it appears.

Buddha

This section provides the foundation of Buddha Heart Parenting. In essence we learn what it is to be an engaged

Buddhist following the Eightfold path. The key Buddhist concepts as they apply to our role as parents are explained and we see how we can eliminate mental afflictions and gain inner peace.

- **Foundation for Buddha Heart Parenting**

- **Our Delusional Way of Operating and How to Change It**

Foundation for Buddha Heart Parenting

Someone asked "What do you mean by the true Buddha, the true dharma, and the true path? Will you please explain them to us?" The Teacher answered, "Buddha is the simple purity of mind. Dharma is the radiant illumination of mind. The path is the clean light that can never be hindered. These three are actually one, yet remain mere names without essence."
Linji Yixuan Ninth Century

How do we combine Buddhism and parenting to engage in Buddha Heart Parenting? The key step is laying the foundations. We need to have a strong base within ourselves from which to operate and see the world. Therefore what we need is a working knowledge of the Buddhist worldview. In this chapter we will explore the fundamental understandings that are necessary to engage in Buddha Heart Parenting.

We need to see things as they really are, not how we think they are. In Buddhism this 'not seeing things as they really are' is called *ignorance*. It is ignorance of the Dharma, ignorance of right knowledge. Ignorance is simply 'not knowing'.

We need to have an intellectual understanding of impermanence, emptiness, dependent origination, mindfulness and equanimity. These concepts will be discussed in later Chapters. We need to follow the Gradual Path to Enlightenment (Lam Rim) and the Eightfold Path. These two are ways of formulating the Buddha's teachings. They are compatible and enable us to look at the same thing from different perspectives. The Lam Rim includes the eight-fold path.

For our purposes I will outline the Eightfold Path and encourage you to read and study the Lam Rim to broaden your understanding and practice.

The Eightfold Path is the fourth noble truth. It provides a lesson plan in wisdom, ethics and meditative skill and allows us the realisation within our deepest consciousness of the Oneness of all life.

With this as our base we can truly engage in Buddha Heart Parenting.

What is the Eightfold Path?

The eight aspects of the path are not to be understood as a sequence of single steps, instead they are highly interdependent

> *Monks, just as a pot without a stand is easy to tip over,*
> *And a pot with a stand is hard to tip over,*
> *So too the mind without a stand is easy to tip over,*
> *And a mind with a stand is hard to tip over.*
> *And what is the mind's stand?*
> *Just this noble eightfold path.*
>   Samyutta Nikaya XLV 27

principles that have to be seen in relationship with each other. The eight aspects give us direction in the following areas of our practice

Wisdom – knowing what will bring beneficial results;
Ethical Action -knowing how to act; and
Mental Training – building strength of mind.

Wisdom. When we know what will bring a beneficial result, then we can form our intention or motivation through this wisdom. Right view refers to the cognitive aspect of wisdom;

right intention refers to the kind of mental energy that controls our actions.

1. **Right View.** Right view is the beginning and the end of the path, and put simply it means to see and to understand things as they really are. We need to understand the interdependence of all phenomena, including self. We can understand this in Buddhist terms as impermanence. Right view means that we keep ourselves free from prejudice, judgement and delusion and begin to see the true nature of life. We can see our children and their behaviour within this view. We also need to understand how karma works, and how we reap what we sow.

2. **Right Intention.** Right intention can be described as commitment to ethical and mental self-improvement. We can work towards developing the right attitude and motivation. Knowledge needs to be linked to personal conviction and intention if any progress is to be made.

Ethical Action. The next three aspects deal with knowing how to act.

3. **Right Speech.** The importance of speech in the context of Buddhist ethics is clear. Words can make enemies or friends, start wars or create peace. Right speech means to refrain from pointless and harmful talk – to speak kindly and courteously to all. Right speech is compassionate communication. Using compassionate communication we look deeply within ourselves and within others.
Without right speech we can start or prolong power struggles with our children, reinforce their inappropriate attempts to meet their needs. Right speech can support our children and help them to reach their potential and get in touch with their own Buddha heart.

4. **Right Action.** Right action refers to the positive non-speech behaviours that we choose to engage in. It means to

make sure our actions benefit others and do not cause harm to their life, health, property and relationships. Right action is living the Dharma daily.

5. **Right Livelihood.** Right livelihood means to follow a line of work that does not harm others and that leads to a development of the other aspects of the path.

Mental Training. The next three aspects deal with mental training.

6. **Right Effort.** Right effort means to direct our efforts continually to overcome ignorance. We need to develop a level of perseverance that is maintained over time. It is a constant process of being aware of mental states and taking action to influence them. This can be difficult because we are attempting to change habituated ways of thinking. Our current thinking is comfortable, so in challenging it we will feel discomfort.

   Even when engaging in right effort, we may work in fits and starts – high motivation, then low or no motivation. This is natural. Progress is often two steps forwards and one step backwards. We need to have compassion for ourselves and not judge our progress. We will get there.

7. **Right Mindfulness.** Right mindfulness means to develop a continual awareness of one's own state and one's environment. It is the mental ability to see things as they are, with clear consciousness. With right mindfulness we can, amongst other things, check our motivation.

8. **Right Concentration.** Right concentration means to concentrate on anything that will help us to see the Oneness of all life and the Buddhahood that exists within all beings. With right concentration we can come to see the Buddha within our children – that they have the pure nature of Buddha deep within the outer coverings of ignorance.

With this understanding it is much easier to engage in Buddha Heart Parenting.

Most steps on the path contain concepts that are easy to understand and put into action.

Some key Buddhist concepts

There are three concepts that are integral to the Buddhist psychology of the mind, which are not so easy to understand. These are impermanence, emptiness, and mindfulness. Let's look at these concepts in more detail.

What is impermanence?

Impermanence is not just another philosophical concept. It is a tool that helps us in our transformation and in our parenting. Acknowledging impermanence is acknowledging that everything changes. But that is not all. Because mind and matter change from moment to moment they therefore have no fixed identity or permanent self. It is because of this changing self that everything is possible. Life itself is possible. Because of impermanence our children will grow into adults. We can be happy in this miracle of impermanence.

Understanding impermanence helps us go beyond all concepts; beyond same and different; coming and going; good and bad; right and wrong. When we look at a river and then look again a moment later, what we see is different. The water in the river is different, the river is not the same river but it is also not different either.

So impermanence can be understood in these terms but we also need to understand impermanence in the light of inter-being. All things inter-are. All things are constantly relying on other things for their existence and all things are constantly influencing other things. We have all heard the saying that when a butterfly flaps its wings on one side of the planet it will affect the weather on the other side. Nothing can exist by itself alone – it depends on every other thing. Things cannot just be, they can only inter-be.

So how do we put our understanding of impermanence and inter-being into practice and how can we use it to parent through our Buddha Heart?

With knowledge of impermanence in our worldview how can we not see through our children's behaviour to see their Buddha heart!

We need to look deeply and see the nature of impermanence, not just the intellectual understanding of the concept. Having grasped this we need to keep it in our consciousness, concentrate on it. Let it become part of our daily being and then, with practice, part of our very being and the object of some of our meditation. In this way the practice of impermanence will grow and become a key that opens the door of reality.

Most of the time we behave with our children as if we had no understanding of impermanence. We tend to act as if they will always be at home with us, whereas it will be only a short number of years before they will leave us to live elsewhere and have a family of their own. We forget to value and treasure the moments we have with our children. When we understand impermanence and take the understanding into our daily life and see how it relates to our life as parents we can never be angry with our children or too busy to spend time with them, listen to them, and play with them.

Some of us may feel sad when we think of impermanence and how things will change within our family and how our children will grow up, but because of impermanence everything is possible. Our freedom, peace and joy in the present moment are the most important things we have and without an understanding of impermanence we will not feel this freedom, peace and joy, but will be looking to the next moment to bring us fulfilment. Therefore without an awakened understanding of impermanence we cannot be truly happy.

What is emptiness?

An understanding of impermanence leads to an understanding of emptiness and its implications. According to Buddhist philosophy, individual things, however we talk of them conventionally, do not have an inherent existence. Their form is temporary. They lack a permanent self – it is the conventional, or dependently arisen self that exists. Emptiness is simply the recognition that nothing has independent selfhood, nothing can exist on its own, everything is interconnected. Emptiness is not a 'something' that lies behind phenomena, it is simply a reminder that nothing is independent and existing from its own side.

Understanding impermanence and emptiness can lead us to skilful means, that is, the understanding can lead us to either methods we follow on our path leading to the realisation of absolute truth (emptiness) and compassion or it leads us to methods that can help someone else to achieve this realisation.

What does it mean to be mindful?

Mindfulness is the seventh step on the Eightfold Path and is key to Buddhist mental training. If everything that happens is a result of causes and conditions, it is important to be aware of exactly what is happening and of our feeling and thoughts in response to what is happening. Mindfulness is a quality of mind that can strengthen our awareness of the causes and conditions determining this present moment, and our awareness of how we are relating to these causes and conditions.

If we want to change our habits, and patterned responses to our children's behaviour, we need this sort of mindful awareness. This way we can be aware of the arising, for instance, of annoyance, and be fully aware of it, instead of responding to it inappropriately, such as by wanting to get rid of it through changing the external environment.

To be aware of our feelings, and their causes in terms of met or unmet needs, gives us an opportunity to decide how we will respond instead of being under the control of those feelings and our patterned response to those feelings. This provides us with a momentary gap between experience and response, and this gap allows us the opportunity to influence our own karma and future, and the karma and future of our children. It is in the enlarged gap (between experience and response) that we can decide which response is skilful or appropriate and beneficial (in the Buddhist sense) to both our child and ourselves.

Some Buddhists talk of using this gap to mentally wish the person happiness. We can do this too. When we first see someone, before we think any other thought, we can send them the thought: 'I wish you happiness.' We may find it difficult at first to make this the first thing we think when we see someone. This is really good practice.

Practicing mindfulness in a positive way has another bonus. Lasting happiness can arise from mindfulness. When we practice mindfulness we can see and appreciate the many things that we see, hear, touch, smell and do that are a source of joy. We see and appreciate the blessed life we share with our children.

We all need to live mindfully in the moment. This means that we need to be clear in our minds just what we want to be mindful about. We can ask ourselves 'What do I want to be mindful of at this moment?' Let's say that our aim is to be mindful of an action. If we then think 'I am being mindful' we are no longer mindful of the action, but instead, we are being mindful of the motivation. We have lost the focus of our mindfulness. Mostly our minds are just like that. We want to be mindful of something, but then the mind switches to another thing, and then another. When we practice mindfulness, not switching the mind, it can be a great relief from all this activity.

This distinction is an important point to consider when understanding mindfulness. It helps us understand that mindfulness, just like other actions, can be appropriate or inappropriate.

When we are interacting with our children – we need to 'be there'. – to stay with our chosen focus. If we choose to play for the joy and delight of playing with our child we need to just play, not play and think about what we will cook for dinner or whether we are teaching the child anything in the playing – just play. What greater joy is there than that?

We can practice mindfulness with everyday activities like eating or cleaning our teeth. The more we practice appropriate mindfulness the easier it will become.

Have you ever had a Murphy's Law Day? One of those days when it seems everything that could go wrong has gone wrong? What is happening is that many negative karmic seeds ripen in one day making that day difficult to deal with. On days like this we often forget to be appropriately mindful, instead we tend to be inappropriately mindful and focus on resentment or frustration or self-pity. Our thoughts may be something like 'Why me? How could this happen?' This leads to unskilful thoughts, speech and actions, and needless to say more negative karmic seeds being sown.

If we can stop ourselves from throwing appropriate mindfulness out the window and reacting to the happenings around us, we will be able to turn it all around. When our children are behaving like terrors of the deep with a vengeance, to see just where our breaking point is, it is difficult to rein in our rampant feelings. But if we have been practicing with the little things on a daily basis, we will, at some point in the Murphy's Law Day, be in touch with what is really happening and be able to change to appropriate mindfulness.

Remember, it is our reaction to what is happening, not what is happening that causes us problems, suffering or happiness. The things that are happening are just that – things that are happening. If we allow these things to influence how we feel and behave, we are giving control of how we feel and behave to the external environment. It is much better to have internal control through maintaining mindfulness of what is happening and to reside in equanimity (evenness of mind or calm). From this position we are better able to support our children and other people. And it feels much better too.

If we can accept responsibility for what we feel and recognise that to get rid of these feelings we have to change something on our inside, we are more than half way there already. It is important to acknowledge and respect our feelings and not deny them. They are our key to self-understanding and change. Our feelings often point towards faulty thinking and faulty beliefs. For example, we may think that we need the approval of others or that how our children behave is a reflection on us. Our feelings guide our inner transformation.

Accepting responsibility for our feelings and working to transform them doesn't mean we do nothing in situations where our children are behaving inappropriately. Sometimes it may be appropriate to say and do nothing but at other times we may need to say or do something so our children can learn effective and productive behaviours.

How can we develop patience?

When our children act like they don't like us, don't respect us, when they are uncooperative, and when they do all they can to press our buttons, it is essential that we have patience, that is, the ability to remain indifferent to the harm inflicted by others. Patience is not the suppression of anger but the ability to remain calm and feel at ease. Buddhist teachings provide us with many tools to help us develop patience. Understanding impermanence, emptiness and mindfulness allows us to practice patience because this understanding helps us to see reality as it is, not how we think it is. It allows us to separate our feelings from what is happening and to remain calm. If we add an understanding of karma we can easily remain calm and compassionate in the midst of chaos.

'Karma' literally means action. The law of karma is the law of cause and effect. For every cause there is an effect and for every effect there is a cause. No action can be taken without there being a resultant effect. An action is any conscious thought, word or deed. Thoughts govern words and deeds. Anything we do is preceded by thoughts – sometimes only a fraction of a second separates them but there is always a conscious thought first. Exceptions are reflexive movements such as striking the tendon below the kneecap, which results in our lower leg jerking forwards. We do not consciously think about jerking our lower leg before it moves – it moves without our conscious thought. According to Buddhist teachings even reflexive movements have an element of awareness in them, but not conscious thought.

In Western language we use the word 'karma' quite freely and often incorrectly. It is often used to mean only the bad effects from some wrong behaviour. But karma has no value judgement attached to it. It is neither good nor bad, it is just karma. Similarly the effects of our actions are neither good nor bad. They might be pleasant or unpleasant but they are not good or bad.

When an effect comes into existence it is said to be the ripening of the karmic seed we planted by our actions in the past, either in this life or a previous life. Everything that happens to us is a result of ripening karmic seeds. The type of child we have is a result of our past karma. Our habitual reactions are determined by past karma. Our external conditions are the ripening result of our karma. And remember our response to the happenings right now, creates karmic seeds that will ripen in the future given the right conditions. This is important for us to realise because it gives us control of our future.

There are two ways of approaching our negative feelings. We can apply Buddhist teachings and practices after we feel them to gain a correct view of things or we can apply Buddhist teachings and practices so that the necessary conditions for the karmic seeds to ripen do not come into being. Just as a plant seed needs the right conditions to germinate (ripen) i.e. water, soil, nutrients, correct temperature, so too do our karmic seeds need the appropriate conditions. If we live as an engaged

Buddhist we prevent the conditions necessary for much of our unpleasant karmic seeds to ripen both for ourselves and for our children. Our children's behaviour may still be inappropriate but we will not react emotionally to it. We will see it for what it really is, and we will be able to maintain equanimity, that is, we will be able to maintain the love we feel for our child simply because they are our child. We will see things as they really are.

How the understanding develops

Equanimity is the basis for unconditional, altruistic love, compassion and joy for other's happiness. Though this process of *equanimity*, loving-kindness, or heart-warming love, can arise. We will see all beings as very pleasant and pleasing. Loving-kindness is not the same as love. The difference may appear subtle. 'Loving-kindness sees all sentient beings as kind and feels warmly towards them, and responds compassionately, wanting them to have happiness and its causes and to be free from suffering. 'Love' simply wishes another to have happiness and its causes, without the compassionate response to try to achieve this. Thus 'loving-kindness' has loving action in mind. Loving-kindness leads to compassionate action.

> Equanimity means having an even-minded approach to all things: unbiased, loving all people with the same powerful love we have for our own children

The foundations for effective Buddha Heart Parenting are understanding impermanence, emptiness and mindfulness along with practicing patience and heart-warming love. They are all interrelated and build on each other. Knowledge of impermanence and emptiness allows us to practice mindfulness skilfully. This in turn leads to patience and the development and expression of heart-warming love. If we combine this with the guiding aspects of the Eightfold path we cannot help but parent through our Buddha heart.

It is one thing to have the worldview and motivation to engage in Buddha Heart Parenting. Now, in the next chapter we need to add to this some concrete strategies based on Buddhist philosophy to change how we react to your children's inappropriate behaviour. After that I will outline further practical strategies we can use to support our children in their change from inappropriate behaviour when their needs are not met, to appropriate behaviour that arises when their needs are met. In this way, our children can get in touch with their true Buddha heart.

Our Delusional Way Of Operating and How to Change It

"Transient are all conditioned things":
When this, with wisdom, one discerns,
Then is one disgusted with ill;
This is the path to purity.
Dhammapada – Maggavagga-The Path, Verse 277.

Remember when we looked at why children behave how they do, we found that behaviour is determined by needs and we saw the importance of not looking at the behaviour *per se* but to look deeply within the child to understand the feeling or emotion and the need. Similarly, any negative emotion

> **Feeling vs Emotions.**
> Feeling, in Buddhism refers to the physical or mental sensations of pleasure, pain and neutral.
> *Emotions* are secondary reactions to the feeling of pleasure, pain or neutral. The mental factors in Buddhism include much of what we mean by emotion. See below.

we have when our child behaves inappropriately is a key indicator of which of our own needs is not being met. This process does not validate our emotions or show that we 'should' have these emotions. The process provides a way of determining our need and theirs in order for us to know how best to respond. Our aim is to help our child learn appropriate behaviours and appropriate beliefs about themselves.

We use labels without realising it

Our emotions when our child behaves inappropriately are a very real indication of our state of mind and our state of spiritual development at that time. The instant we see, feel or hear something we label it as pleasant, unpleasant or neutral. Feelings arise from the label, although they can arise without conscious labelling. Let's look at the labels and feelings.

When the label of **pleasant** is given to an object or action, we tend to develop **attachment** because we like it – it pleases us – and we want to be around it or to have it happen again, and again.

When the label of **unpleasant** is given to an object or action, we can develop **aversion** (or **anger**), because we want it to stop or go away. We may even develop hatred.

When the label of **neutral** is given to an object or action, we really don't care if it is there or not. Often we won't even consciously be aware of it.

The process of labelling usually takes only a fraction of a second to occur, and sometimes we aren't even aware we are doing it. Once we have labelled an object or action as unpleasant or bad, we see 'bad' as the inherent quality of the object or action. In this way we label our child's behaviour as bad, and sometimes we label our child as bad as well. But it is clear to all of us that there are some people who would not label this behaviour in the same way – they might have more patience and might not be bothered by these things. Therefore the behaviour (or the child) cannot be 'good' or 'bad' it is just a subjective opinion of our mind – an opinion that was formed at first glance.

Not only do we label, but we habituate the label as well. Habituation comes to the fore to reinforce our opinions and prejudices. Habituation is not all negative – the Tibetan word for meditation means 'familiarity, which can be a positive habituation'. Our opinions about our child and our child's behaviour can become habituated. Once something is a habit, we no longer question our behaviour – it becomes automatic and very difficult to change. This is beneficial if positive behaviour has become habituated, for example, if we automatically think of how to make others happy. But it is very damaging when negative behaviour has become ingrained.

A story told by the Buddha to show how some habituation can result in closed-mindedness:

> *A young widower, who loved his five year old son very much, was away on business when bandits came who burned down the whole village, killed several occupants, and took his son away. When the man returned, he saw the ruins and panicked. He took the corpse of a small child to be his son and cried uncontrollably. He organised a cremation ceremony, collected the ashes and put them in a beautiful little bag that he always kept with him.*
>
> *Soon afterwards, his real son escaped from the bandits and found his way home. He arrived at his father's new cottage at midnight and knocked on the door. His father, still grieving asked: "Who is it?". The child answered, "It is me papa, open the door!" But believing his son to be dead, the father thought that some young boy was making fun of him. He shouted: "Go away" and continued to cry.*
>
> *After some time the child left. Father and son never saw each other again.*

After telling this story, the Buddha said:

> *"Sometime, somewhere, you take something to be the truth. If you cling to it so much, even when the truth comes in person and knocks on your door, you will not open it."*

Delusional emotions are labels

The labels we apply in that first instant, or that become habituated motivate us to act inappropriately. These labels are not based on reality.

When delusions arise within our mental continuum, these states of mind leave us disturbed, confused, and unhappy.

> **Emotion** in Buddhist terms is a mental state that starts the instant the mind judges (feels attachment vs. aversion; sees good vs. bad, them vs. us or me etc), and may happen long before the normal person is conscious of it. Emotion arises from the habitual clinging that makes us automatically judge our experiences according to whether we (or our ego) find them attractive (attachment), unattractive (anger), or neutral (ignorance). The more clinging there is, the stronger our reactions will be, until we reach a point where they finally break into our conscious mind and manifest as the obvious feelings we usually call emotions.

Because they afflict us in this way or delude us they are called 'afflictive emotions' or 'delusions'.

The most important delusional emotions are often referred to as the Three Poisons and are **ignorance, anger** or **strong aversion,** and **attachment.** Some texts refer to six poisons or delusional emotions or mental afflictions: anger, attachment, ignorance, jealousy and pride, and wrong views, but the three primary ones are anger, attachment and ignorance. We also have many more delusional emotions in addition to these five and they all underlie one or more of these three main ones.

Our psychological needs arise from these poisons or mental afflictions. Without the mental afflictions we wouldn't have the psychological needs.

Some of these terms used in Buddhism sometimes have slightly different meanings from what we have in the English language, which may be confusing. In this book, I most often use the terms with their Buddhist meaning, but I do, on occasion, use them with their usual English language meaning. The context will make it clear. Here are the Buddhist meanings for some terms used in this book.

Ignorance refers to the Buddhist concept of lack of wisdom, or lack of insight into the actual way that things exist i.e. not knowing impermanence and emptiness. It can be a 'not knowing' of anything, such as not knowing how to apply resuscitation. Ignorance is not something neutral without effects or consequences; it is a definite state of mind and feeling which causes us to act in a certain way.

Ignorance is the root of all afflictions - it underpins attachment and anger. There are two kinds of ignorance:

• The ignorance of not knowing reality – ranging from simple 'not knowing' such as not knowing how to drive a car, to 'not knowing what is behind our suffering – 'not knowing' why we are angry, and 'not knowing' the meaning of karmic cause and effect, etc; and

• Self-grasping ignorance – this is the ignorance that believes that we exist from our own side. We project this inherent existence onto our body and mind. We do not exist in this projected way (which is what is meant by selflessness or emptiness) but we do still exist. We exist as a result of causes and effects, that is, we exist as a dependent arising and we are interconnected with all phenomena.

When we gain wisdom we no longer have ignorance. This means we no longer have the delusions that arise from that ignorance. With wisdom we see clearly. We can act appropriately, without mistakes. If I am ignorant about resuscitation methods, then I may be unable to save a drowning child. Once that ignorance is removed, I have the wisdom that knows resuscitation, I can act appropriately and the child's life may be saved.

Aversion arises when we want to be separated from someone or something (eg some behaviour), which we do not like, that is from the label of 'unpleasant'. This label is very relative and based on limited information, and so aversion arises from an aspect of exaggeration or 'projection'. **Anger** is defined as the desire to harm, particularly to harm the person who is deemed to be preventing us from having the object of our desire. Anger is aversion with stronger exaggeration.

Attachment is an exaggerated not wanting to be separated from someone or something, including a situation or a behaviour that we like – that we have labelled 'pleasant'. In the Four Noble truths, Buddha Shakyamuni taught that attachment to self is the root cause of suffering. If we don't have attachments, naturally we will experience less suffering.

> *There was an old cultivator who asked for instructions from a monk, "Great Monk, let me ask you, how can I attain liberation?" The Great Monk said, "Who tied you up?" The old cultivator answered, "Nobody tied me up." The monk said, "Then why do you seek liberation?"*
>
> Hsuan Hua, tr., Flower Adornment Sutra,
> "Pure Conduct," chap. 11

In fact we have tied ourselves up with the knots of ignorance, attachment and aversion. It is from our attachment to self that attachments to outside things, events, situations etc arise. Because we see ourselves as separate independent entities, we usually have attachment to what is seen to be pleasurable, and aversion to what is not. If we no longer have attachment to self then we no longer crave or desire pleasure. What is pleasurable in one instant is not in the next. Nothing is permanent. How does this work?

Understanding impermanence is a key to eliminating attachment. The source of all delusions is a distorted awareness called 'self-grasping ignorance', which grasps phenomena as inherently or independently existent. Whereas all phenomena are dependent arisings. That is, their existence is utterly dependent on other phenomena, such as their causes, their parts, and the minds that apprehend them. Objects do not exist from their own side, in and of themselves. What objects are, depends on how they are viewed. It is our failure to realise this that is the source of all our problems.

The kind of self-grasping that harms us the most is when we instinctively feel that we possess a completely real and objective self or that we exist independently of all other phenomena. One consequence of this grasping at self as separate is that we develop self-cherishing – a mind that regards our self as supremely important. This causes us to be drawn to people, situations, etc that we find pleasurable and we want to be separate from things we find unpleasurable. This is the birth of attachment, anger/aversion and indifference. When we have this exaggerated sense of our own importance we feel that other's interests are in conflict with our own. We want our children to behave in such a way that makes us feel good – because self-grasping attachment says what we want is more important than what they want.

> *From attachment springs grief, from attachment springs fear; for him who is wholly free from attachment there is no grief, whence fear?*
> Dhammapada – Pyavagga-Affection, Verse 214.

The word 'poison' is used because these reactions poison our mind and prevent the appearance of its intrinsic wisdom.

How can we eliminate negative emotions?

Buddhism shows us ways to eliminate the Three Poisons or negative states of mind of ignorance, anger/aversion, and attachment. The negative emotions of the human beings in the 21st century are the same as the negative emotions of people at the time of the Buddha, or in the 3rd century or the 15th century.

Although all three poisons or delusions are interrelated it can be helpful to deal with them in turn.

How can we get rid of ignorance?

Ignorance can be removed through study, meditation, and reflection, that is, by developing wisdom. Understanding the concepts of cause and effect, impermanence, emptiness, and other core Buddhist principles provides us with access to wisdom to remove ignorance.

How can we get rid of anger?

Anger is the most obvious of the Three Poisons. When we are angry we know it – it is an unmistakable feeling. When it builds, anger can feel like we are almost out of control. Similarly, when someone else is feeling anger, we are usually able to detect it.

> *It is natural for the immature to harm others. Getting angry with them is like resenting a fire for burning.*
>
> Shantideva.

When we feel negative emotion/feeling and blame the outside world for creating them we may choose to become angry in an attempt to change the external environment to make the feeling or emotion go away. For example, we may shout at our child and demand they clean up their mess. We may punish her so we won't feel like this again. If our child says something to hurt us we want, and demand, an apology. When we think we need the big guns to get some change we may become physically violent. If we listen to our internal dialogue and are mindful of what is going on inside our mind we will know just what we are doing.

> *Holding on to anger is like grasping a hot coal with the intent of throwing it at someone else; you are the one who gets burned.*
>
> Buddha

Anger is a wish to inflict harm either through a physical action, words or thoughts. We do all these things in order to change the external environment. But it is not the external environment that we need to change, - it is the internal. It is our attachment to the status quo that causes the emotion. After all, a messy room is just that – a messy room. Words of defiance are just that – words. Refusal to do what we want is just that – refusal. How these things impact on us is our choice. They are not causing our emotion – we are!

If the child's actions were causing the emotion, then everyone would have exactly the same emotion – and to the same degree – as we do. This is not the case. Some people don't mind a messy house at all. Some parents may be mildly annoyed at words of defiance and refusal to follow their instructions, while others would not be bothered at all. Clearly, we are causing our emotion.

Put anger away, abandon pride,
Overcome every attachment,
Cling not to Mind and Body
And thus be free from sorrow.
          Dhammapada – Kodhavagga-Anger, Verse 221.

Some people think that anger is beneficial. Or they think that our anger is justified. That if we didn't get angry our children would walk all over us. But if we look deeper, are we happy when we are annoyed, irritated, angry or raging? The answer is **No**. No one is happy when they have these emotions. And if we aren't happy when we're angry, how can anger be positive? Positive qualities bring happiness. Negative ones do not.

Other people think we should suppress our anger – that it is OK to feel it but not OK to express it. Buddhist teachings don't advocate suppressing anger. The aim is to not feel it at all. Not just: 'Don't let it show', but don't feel it in the first place.

Many therapists advocate beating pillows or screaming in solitude. Some call this "getting in touch with our anger". But these actions are aggressive, either physically aggressive or verbally aggressive. These actions can habituate aggressive responses to feelings of anger and they reinforce its uprising.

So, if suppressing anger or letting it out are not appropriate, what is? The Buddha advocates dissolving anger so it no longer exists.

How do we dissolve anger? There are seven tools outlined below that can help us dissolve anger.

Use Wisdom

If we deeply realise the emptiness of inherent existence or interdependence of all beings (including the person we are angry with), the situation and oneself, there is nothing to be angry about. Therefore the realisation of emptiness is the ultimate means of ridding ourselves of unrealistic negative emotions such as anger.

Understand the need

When we feel anger we can look deeply in our mind to see what is happening. When we understand that emotion is determined by met or unmet needs, we can look beyond the emotion to find the need. When we understand the need behind the anger we are in a better position to dissolve the anger, and take action to have our need met. The need that we identify may not be obvious. Sometimes we become angry when a seemingly little thing happens, but the anger is caused by something else. The little thing was just the last straw. Until we look deeply we may miss the real need that is unmet. Understanding the need is one way of practicing patience.

Practice Meditation

Buddhism offers us techniques for eliminating anger: the practice of patience, compassion, and mindfulness, reflection and honest observation of one's own mind. Meditation is an ideal method to review a situation in which we became angry. Regular meditation gives us an understanding of what anger is and what happens to us when we are angry. With this understanding gained in the meditation practice we can then gradually apply it in real-life situations. In meditation we can re-run the mental video of when we became angry with our children and then apply different techniques to it whilst still in meditation. In this way we can shape and habituate our skilful behaviour and response to our children's behaviour. Insights gained in meditation help us to view the situation from a new perspective and with that, the anger decreases.

Develop Compassion & Patience

To combat and subdue anger we need to develop a compassionate mind. We need to have the compassion for our children that comes from wisdom. Often what we think of as compassion is not compassion at all, but is sympathy. Sympathy can lead to disempowering actions that do not benefit our children.

We need to ask ourselves: 'Is the child happy?' If they are angry or destructive or aggressive etc they are obviously not happy. That's why they are acting this way. All of us know what it feels like to be unhappy. We need to put ourselves in our child's shoes – how would we like others to react? Mostly we want them to understand us and help us. We need to feel compassion – not anger. When we feel compassion, our hearts are filled with patience and loving-kindness – no matter how our child behaves.

Our attitude changes when we see the situation from their perspective and understand their need, instead of seeing it from our own self-centred perspective. This does not mean we let our child do whatever she likes. Being compassionate does not mean being passive or permissive. If we use anger when disciplining we harm the child and ourselves. To discipline means to teach and when we teach with compassion and wisdom we may be firm, but we remain calm and are able to communicate with our child.

We also need compassion for ourselves. If we become angry with ourselves for having anger at our children or their behaviour, we will have two angers at the same time. We only have to observe our anger with love and attention and it will transform itself. If we are peaceful in ourselves, we can make peace with our anger. We can deal with all other unpleasant feelings such as anxiety or fear in the same way.

When we transform anger by looking and working within; our anger becomes another kind of energy – understanding and compassion.

Gain Inner Peace

We all want peace in the world. But to have world peace we must first have inner peace. To realise/actualise peace in the future is to realise/actualise peace in the present moment. When we know how to be peace, all our transactions with our children are skilful and will give them a greater potential – we will serve our children in a positive way when we act skilfully.

Practice Mindfulness

Mindfulness is our tool for recognising feelings and emotions as they arise. Through mindfulness we can hold the emotion with love and this results in calming down the emotion. We can then identify the need that is driving the emotion.

View our child as ...

An effective way to eliminate our anger or annoyance is to imagine our child as something other than what we are seeing at the time of our negative emotions. There are many different ways to do this. I suggest you find one, or ones, that you feel comfortable with and that work for you. Here are three that may be useful.

1. **Teacher/Supporter.** Without the existence of our child and the behaviour that has triggered our anger and annoyance, how can we learn patience? Without realising the perfection of patience we cannot attain enlightenment. Our child is giving us the opportunity to put the teachings of the Buddha into practice. Therefore, just as the Buddha is kind and precious, so too is our child. We need to have gratitude towards our child. When we start to feel anger or annoyance, we can mentally thank our child and feel grateful that they have provided us with the opportunity to develop our practice.
2. **Mother or supporter.** According to Buddhist thinking, our children have been our mother in previous lives. They have also been our supporters and nurturers. If we think that

they have been our mother in a previous life, and that in that life they loved us, nurtured us and did all they were able to in order for us to be happy, then we can see them in a different light. We can love them like a mother and repay the kindness they showed us in that life.

3. **Buddha.** Because of rebirth, it is possible that our child is a Buddha or highly enlightened being who has chosen to be reborn as our child so that they may help us to achieve enlightenment. Their behaviour is providing you with the necessary opportunities to achieve enlightenment. We do not know that our child is not a fully-realised Buddha taking the role of errant child for our ultimate benefit. How can we know? They are not going to tell us. If they did, the opportunities would not be there for us. Viewing the other person as a Buddha is one of the most powerful tools for dealing with, not only our own children, but all sentient beings.

How can we get rid of attachment?

Attachment may appear to be much less destructive than anger but it is just as destructive. Anger is relatively easy to transform or rid ourselves of, but attachment is harder to abandon because we like to indulge in fantasies.

Anger is also easy to notice. We know when we feel anger. Attachment is much harder to recognise and harder to abandon because we like our attachments. Attachment can lead to anger when we feel we are going to lose the object of our attachment.

Here is an example of how attachment can lead to distorted views and anger at our children:

Shaun has had a difficult childhood. He suffered physical and psychological abuse from both his parents for much of his developing years. Now as a father of four young children he is finding it very hard to put into practice effective parenting skills. He and his partner have attended two parenting courses, and Shaun feels he knows the skills. But in everyday life, these skills go out the window. He is highly motivated to change his parenting practices but something is stopping him. He compounds the issue by giving himself a very hard time for his mistakes. As a practicing Buddhist he believes his actions are unskilful and are causing harm to his children. He also believes he is planting karmic seeds that will ripen in the future when the conditions are right, and that when this happens this will be unpleasant for him. But still he seems unable to stop himself.

Shaun's situation illustrates that to know what to do, and why, is not enough. He is experiencing the ripening of previously sown karmic seeds. If he changes the conditions that are allowing or causing them to ripen, he will be able to change his parenting and implement more effective skills.

*Shaun also needs to develop his mind – follow the Dharma teachings. When he reflects on a deeper level he is able to identify that his parenting skills go out the window chiefly in two situations. Firstly, if Shaun is stressed, his tolerance level drops markedly. The house **must** be neat and tidy and his timetable **must** hold. This makes it difficult for his partner, whose approach to life is more laidback. Shaun is an exceptionally organised person and runs a large company. At work he can maintain control. Things run the way he wants them to. At home, if things are not organised and scheduled he feels threatened. In Shaun's early childhood, he discovered that his security lay in his ability to organise the things around him. He could not rely on his father to provide emotional or physical security so he set about ensuring some level of security in that unstable environment. Now as an adult and father he tries to maintain his security and stability in the same way at home. When things are not organised and going to plan he will become impatient with his children and nag, scold, shout, and punish to make sure the order prevails.*

It is Shaun's attachment to order in the external environment that causes the difficulties. His desire to maintain a tidy household as well as his schedule of activities, also means that he must have control. And if this control is threatened he gets angry – angry at his partner and angry at his children. The desire for control is heightened if he tells one of his children to do something or to stop doing something and the child refuses. The situation usually escalates to unpleasant control and defiance, with raised voices and threats on both sides.

Shaun could benefit from going within and making friends with his mind and gaining an understanding of what his mind is doing. Calm abiding meditation and self-compassion could help him to act more skilfully. He would find this easier if he could let go of his attachment to perfect living conditions and the need to control. In meditation he can look at the attachment for what it is - a grasping for temporary pleasure. This grasping is not only useless, it creates many problems, and karmic actions that are better avoided.

Just like Shaun, we can benefit from remembering that knowledge, wisdom, and internal transformation occur gradually and that we must persevere with joy, knowing that we can make progress. When a child discovers reading and sometimes expects to be able to read instantly, we understand that this desire is normal but not always realistic. We will suffer less if we are as patient with ourselves as we would be with our child learning to read.

> *"We are the results of what we were,*
> *and we will be the results of what we are."*

What else can we do to release attachment?

Practice non-attachment to objects

As Buddhist practitioners and as parents we must reduce, little by little, our attachment to our household and the world. As a first step in letting go of attachment, we can develop non-attachment to objects. This is often much easier than developing non-attachment to people, situations, behaviours, or developing non-attachment to our own self – self-grasping. We can start by letting go of some of our possessions – we can start with possessions that we don't have a strong attachment to and work up to ones we are strongly attached to. We don't have to literally get rid of them although to get rid of some of our possessions can help. We can imagine we no longer have them and realise that is OK. We can think of all the positive benefits of not having them. No matter what possession we are thinking of, there are benefits of not having them – it may just be difficult to see them because of our attachment to the possession.

Meditate on impermanence and death

If we meditate on impermanence and death it will provide the remedy to the attachment and clinging to this life and all that is in it. This attachment is what brings us all our problems, confusion, obstacles to Dharma practice. This attachment actually prevents our attitude and actions from becoming Dharma. Meditation on impermanence and death becomes our antidote to the delusions.

> *The fire of the three poisons, attachment, anger and ignorance,*
> *Burns up all the forests of virtue;*
> *Those who would tread the Bodhisattva Path,*
> *Should be forbearing in mind and body.*
> *Compassion is the pure and refreshing water that can extinguish the fire of afflictions;*
> *Forbearance is the enduring armour that can block all poisoned arrows;*
> *The Dharma of the Void is the light that can completely destroy the sombre smoke of delusion.*
> *Knowing these things and relying on them to rid ourselves of anger and resentment is to have 'entered the house of the Buddhas, worn the armour of the Buddhas and sat on the Buddhas' throne.*
> > Master Thich Thien Tam

It all starts with our mind

In this Chapter we have looked at the mental delusions or poisons that lie at the heart of all our problems, not just the problems we have with our children. Because of these delusions of attachment, which arise from desire, aversion, which arise from frustrated desire, and ignorance, which is a lack of knowledge, we do not always act skilfully when interacting with our children.

Our mind is the root of the problem. We need to work with our mind. We can use meditation, visualisation, Dharma study, and some of the other techniques outlined in this Chapter. Eliminating mental delusions can take a long time and progress may seem slow at times. Fortunately there are practices and practical methods we can use to parent our children, that support the work we are doing on our mind. The two go hand-in-hand to support each other. While we are developing our mind, we are gaining the skills that reflect the enlightened mind. This leads to much faster progress.

The mind is hard to check.
It is swift and wanders at will.
To control it is good.
A controlled mind is conducive to happiness.
Dhammapada – Cittavagga-The Mind, Verse 35.

Parenting Approaches –
What works and What doesn't

Let your love flow outward through the universe,
To its height, its depth, its broad extent,
A limitless love, without hatred or enmity.
Then as you stand or walk,
Sit or lie down,
As long as you are awake,
Strive for this with a one-pointed mind;
Your life will bring heaven to earth.

Sutta Nipata

In this section we are shown the flaws in some of the popular modern parenting approaches and how some can actually cause more inappropriate behaviour.

- **Behaviour Management and Change Approaches**

Behaviour Management and Change Approaches

In this chapter we firstly look at one of the most common approaches to parenting and we see why some aspects of this approach do not fit with Buddhist philosophy. We will then look at the alternative approaches that can be used in Buddha Heart Parenting – why they are appropriate and how they work.

Of the many behaviour management and change approaches available, the ones applicable to Buddha Heart Parenting are ones that attempt to help our child build a code of ethics and learn skilful responses to everyday situations, based on compassion and wisdom. These are the approaches that also support us, in our Dharma practice.

The most common approach to parenting is behaviour management through punishment and reward, sometimes called positive and negative reinforcement. There are aspects of both reward and punishment that do not fit with Buddhist philosophy, and so are inappropriate. We often use reward and punishment with the best of intentions but without an understanding of their effects. When we know the effects and also know of alternative approaches we are in a better position to choose how we will parent our children.

Why are punishment and reward inappropriate?

The most widely used approaches to parenting are based on punishment and reward. When we think of punishment we sometimes think only of physical punishment, but punishment can be either physical or non-physical. It can involve withdrawal of things or events, or threats, as well as physical pain or discomfort.

In society, 'punishment' is the practice of **imposing** something unpleasant on a **wrongdoer**. To 'punish' means to **inflict** a penalty – to inflict pain, suffering or loss. Punishment involves a judgement about the child or the behaviour as 'bad' or 'wrong', and involves a desire to cause suffering, either physically, psychologically, emotionally or mentally as a way to force the child to change their behaviour. In contrast, Buddha Heart methods are based on compassion and on a desire to support the child in learning skilful actions, and there is never any intention to cause suffering.

It's important to understand this difference, because there are some Buddha Heart skills that rely on us providing consequences for our children's inappropriate behaviour, and if we use them without this understanding, they may be seen by the child as punishment and the risks that come with punishment are present. Understanding this difference can mean the difference between success and failure in achieving our goals. In later sections we look at how we can assert boundaries without the use of punishment.

> *If you judge people,*
> *You have no time to love them.*
>
> Mother Teresa

Apart from the obvious inappropriateness of punishment, there are some practical reasons why we shouldn't use punishment.

1. Punishment moves the focus away from the behaviour, to whether the punishment is fair, and to whether it is enforced.

2. Punishment gives the child someone to be angry at. When children are angry they are not considering the behaviour that is being punished – their focus is on being angry at

their parent. Once the child becomes angry at their parent they consider the parent to be 'wrong' and the child believes they, themselves, are 'right'.

3. Punishment may work in the immediate timeframe in which it is given, but the changed behaviour doesn't last. Research has shown that when punishment stops there is a return to the original behaviour. There is considerable evidence that behaviour change as a result of punishment doesn't translate to situations when the parent is either not present or is not likely to find out about the inappropriate behaviour. So, children may behave appropriately in the home but when they are at a friend's house or somewhere else where they feel sure their parents won't find out about what they do, they will behave differently.

4. Studies have shown that punishment induces behaviour change that is based on fear of being found out, not on what is 'right' or 'wrong'. There are other behaviour change approaches that help the child to build a code of ethics that then holds in all situations, not just when the parent is present.

5. Because punishment induces fear, children will lie to avoid punishment.

6. Punishment can lead to aggressive behaviour. Several studies have found the use of punishment produces aggressive behaviour in children. An inherent feature of punishment is that it can be given only by someone in control, and it is given as a method to maintain control. Physical punishment teaches children that human interaction is based on force, that 'might makes right'. Children learn that if they want someone to do something they (the child) can exert their control over them with punishment i.e. aggressive words or actions, or by withdrawing their contact or affection from that person.

7. Being physically punished throws children into a state of powerful emotional confusion making it difficult for them to learn the lessons adults claim they are trying to teach. If

a parent delivers punishment in anger, the adult's anger is not diminished nor is the child's behaviour improved by the child being punished. In fact, research has shown that adults who used physical punishment – eg a smack – get angrier, and smacked children tend to behave worse.

8. Punishment destroys trust. How could we trust someone who punished us, either physically or non-physically? We can't, neither can children. Punishment results in fear, resentment and mistrust.

9. Punishment creates a 'me' versus 'you' atmosphere. Children whose parents use punishment will often try to see just how much they can get away with before the parent punishes them.

10. Punishment takes the responsibility for appropriate behaviour away from the child and puts it squarely with the parent. When we use punishment, by our actions we have accepted responsibility for our child's behaviour. The parent is the one who judges it to be 'wrong' and the parent is the one to take corrective measures. The child may feel they have no responsibility.

11. Punishment denies our child the right to experience, and learn from, the real effects of their actions. All negative, unskilful behaviour has negative consequences. Often all we need to do is to help our child to see the negative consequences - not to create new ones. Our role as parents is to help our child to know positive alternatives to inappropriate behaviour. Buddha Heart Parenting provides many ways of doing this.

Everything we have talked about so far in relation to punishment applies to both non-physical and physical punishment. Both non-physical and physical punishment are based on producing fear as the deterrent to certain behaviours. Therefore they are both aggressive. Anything that is meant to instil fear is aggressive.

Of course, physical punishment has many more possible

negative effects than non-physical. Longitudinal studies have found that physical (corporal) punishment by parents can result in mental health issues, aggression, and criminal or antisocial behaviour in children. A connection has also been found between the physical punishment of children and the behaviour of those children, as adults, to their own children or spouse - it has been found that they are more likely to abuse their own children or spouse. This doesn't mean that every child that is punished will abuse their children, but it means there is a connection between the two actions.

Rewards can also be counterproductive. If the cessation of negative behaviour is rewarded by a parent, it does not necessarily mean the child has learnt why the behaviour was negative and why it is skilful to cease it. Similarly, positive behaviour can be rewarded without the child internalising why that behaviour is 'positive'. If the rewarder is absent why would the child continue to act appropriately? This issue is discussed later when we look at 'praise vs feedback.

Why behaviour modification fails to benefit our child

Punishment and reward are used as a form of behaviour modification. The behaviour modification approach tries to make a change in a child's external behaviour rather than a change in her inner thoughts and feelings. So behaviour modification is an external environmental conditioning approach – it places all responsibility for the child's behaviour on us, the parent.

Our child is capable of directing her own behaviour. Behaviour modification focuses on the consequences not on the causes of her behaviour. It is important we understand that cause comes before behaviour, while consequence is a result of the behaviour. Behaviour modification as a behaviour change approach is therefore usually not the most appropriate approach to use. This is not to say that behaviour modification does not work. It can work to change behaviour, but it does not support our child to understand cause-effect and to build a code of ethics to guide their behaviour throughout their life. Behaviour modification, though, can achieve results, where other methods have failed, for example with children who are intellectually impaired or autistic.

Continuous reinforcement followed by partial reinforcement is another strategy used in behaviour modification to change a child's behaviour to the desired behaviour. When the child first does the 'right' behaviour, the parent reinforces it with praise or another kind of reward. For a period of time this is continued every time the child does the 'right' behaviour. Then the continuous reinforcement drops back to occasional reinforcement. This is called partial reinforcement. This kind of behaviour modification often works quite well, but, again, it provides an external *locus of control*. Even though the child may learn to always do the 'right' behaviour, they often have not internalised the reason for this. It is not based on their code of ethics. It is based on habit.

> **Locus of control** refers to a person's generalised expectations as to who or what is responsible for what happens. People tend to believe their chances of future success or failure are under the control of either internal or external factors.

In the section below where we talk about consistency I will explain how partial reinforcement can actually entrench inappropriate behaviour.

What is the Buddha Heart behaviour change approach?

Within Buddha Heart Parenting there are a number of strategies and techniques we can use to help our children to modify their behaviour and develop a code of ethics. The most important thing that determines the success of these strategies and techniques is whether we are coming from our Buddha Heart when we use them.

There are some general concepts that relate to behaviour

change that are useful to understand before we get into the nitty-gritty of what to do to support our child's change to appropriate behaviour. If we understand **locus of control, partial reinforcement** and **consistency**, and their effects we are in a much better position to work effectively from our Buddha Heart.

Where is the locus of control?

Locus of control refers to the extent to which a person believes that they can control events that affect them. A person with a high internal locus of control believes events primarily result from their own behaviour and actions. They have a good understanding of cause and effect and of karma and karmic ripening. On the other hand, people with a high external locus of control believe that powerful others, fate or chance primarily determine what happens.

Children who believe that an outcome is largely contingent on their own behaviour are seen as having a more internal locus of control whereas those children who believe that luck, chance or powerful parents largely determine an outcome are considered to have a more external locus of control.

Whether a child sees the locus of control as external or internal, plays a very large role in his/her behaviour. Most behaviour modification approaches use an external locus of control i.e. the parent, to achieve appropriate behaviour. A child may fail to see the connection between their actions and the consequences. Instead, they learn that the parent is in control of the consequences. Therefore they fail to learn appropriate behaviour, simply because they don't know it is appropriate behaviour. Instead they see it as behaviour the parent wants them to engage in.

Research shows that children who have an internal rather than an external locus of control are more likely to have parents who treat them consistently, give them more autonomy and provide a warmer, more supportive and compassionate relationship. In other words, if we treat our children with kindness and compassion, they are more likely to develop an internal locus of control.

Needless to say, Buddha Heart Parenting supports the child to have an internal locus of control and a good understanding of karma and karmic ripening i.e. cause and effect.

Partial reinforcement vs consistency

As parents, one of the most difficult things we have to do, is to be consistent when dealing with our children. We need to be consistent so they know where they stand, so they know we love them, so they know where the boundaries are, and so they feel secure and trust us. This doesn't mean we have to be perfect. We are human, but we need to understand the importance of consistency when we are supporting our children to change inappropriate behaviour.

Partial reinforcement occurs when the child's behaviour is reinforced only sometimes. Behaviour maintained or produced on a partial reinforcement schedule is harder to extinguish than behaviour learned or maintained using continuous reinforcement. This applies to both appropriate and inappropriate behaviour. I often use the example of my children who used to check the coin-return slot of public phones when we were out shopping. Occasionally, perhaps in one in forty phones, they would find some coins in the slot. Despite the infrequency of success, they persisted for many years in checking out the slot in any public phone they saw. This is a really good and easily understood example of how partial reinforcement works.

Here is an example of how partial reinforcement influences inappropriate behaviour. If our child is trying to gain recognition by engaging in inappropriate behaviour we may decide the most appropriate way to help her is to ignore the behaviour. Sometimes we may be successful but other times when the behaviour continues for 20 minutes we feel we can no longer ignore it, so we tell her to stop. At this point she has gained what she wanted – recognition – and we have given her partial reinforcement. What she has learnt from this experience is that if she continues an inappropriate behaviour for long enough, or often enough, we will eventually give in and give her what she is wanting.

Of course, other things influence what our child will do. When we recognise that our child is engaging in inappropriate behaviour because she needs more positive attention, we then give her more quality time. By doing this her need for attention and recognition will be largely met and consequently her inappropriate bid for attention will decrease.

The effectiveness of partial reinforcement can also be seen in adults where the gambling industry relies on it to make money from people who believe they will win eventually, if they just keep going. Perhaps the adults who are susceptible to gambling addiction were once children whose parents used partial reinforcement for their inappropriate behaviour. They learnt that they would eventually get what they wanted if they kept up the behaviour.

When we are attempting to support our children to change their behaviour we need to understand the effects of inconsistency and do our utmost to be consistent. This is often easier to achieve if we break down what we want to do into smaller, easier to accomplish tasks. Instead of attempting to change all our parenting behaviours at once, we may find it easier to change only one or two at a time, and perhaps to work on just one or two of our children's behaviours at a time. When we take on too much we can become discouraged and feel like giving up. Little successes increase our motivation to continue.

But what of consistency between parents? It is quite common for parents to differ in their views on parenting. Is this a problem? In an ideal world, both parents would have similar values and views on how to parent. Parents who agree on boundaries and standards, who convey the same sorts of messages and who value compassion over coercion provide the best foundation for their children's well-being. But this seldom happens. What is important is that the parents can agree to disagree about what is the 'best' way to parent. It is important that parents are not open to manipulation and to playing one parent off against the other. They need to work together as a team and support each other even if they would have handled it differently themselves.

Parents may differ to such an extent in their views of parenting that they have to agree for one parent to take charge of a particular area. For example, mum may take charge of meal times, and dad takes charge of bedtime. This is not the most desirable outcome but it is much better than open conflict and disagreement between the parents with one undermining the other.

Have age appropriate expectations

Much of what we think is our children's inappropriate behaviour is actually age appropriate behaviour. We talked about this earlier. Our job is made easier when we have an awareness of what is appropriate behaviour for the ages of their children. Most books on child development provide descriptions of what to expect from different ages, and can help us be clear on what is age appropriate and what is not.

When we think our child is behaving inappropriately we can stop and think. Is it really inappropriate or is it age-appropriate. Here are some very general expectations.

Birth to 1 year: Babies can't understand or follow instructions. They know what they feel.

1-2 years: They can follow simple instructions, but don't understand the 'why' of many things we ask them to do.

2-3 years: They are now better at talking and listening. Children are too young at this age to share and to play fair without our guidance.

3-5 years: Children need our help to know what is appropriate and what is inappropriate.

Knowing what is appropriate for different age groups can help us to see the world through our children's eyes and helps us to make sure their environment is suitable for them.

The home environment can encourage appropriate behaviour

We can help our child to behave appropriately by arranging their home environment with them in mind. Children need a safe environment where they are able to explore and play without risk of danger or 'don't touch'. They are small for only a short time, and if we have chosen to be parents surely we can rearrange our house and put our 'precious' possessions out of reach for a few short years. Children also need free access to a large enough outside play area that is also safe. The more they can explore and play unhindered the better able they are to learn and grow.

By rearranging our home and garden we are also preventing possible conflict situations from developing between ourselves and our children. A lot of inappropriate behaviour is a result of children being confined in a small area for too long, or is a result of too many restrictions on what they can touch and cannot touch, or can and cannot do.

What are the major strategies of Buddha Heart Parenting?

Buddha Heart Parenting has several core strategies that work with compassion and wisdom to support our child. There are strategies that help our child to learn cause-effect and responsible, compassionate action; to learn to effectively solve their own problems to the higher good of all concerned; to understand and express their feelings; to listen empathically to others and understand their feelings and needs; and there are strategies to support us to meet both our child's needs and our own.

Underlying all the strategies is communication that is compassionate and comes from our Buddha Heart. This compassionate communication is a process of deeply connecting with ourselves and our child. Compassionate communication allows us not only to connect to people at a deep and empathic level, but allows us a way of connecting and expressing our own feelings and needs as well.

In all our interactions with our children a compassionate connection comes first. This connection is at the core of Buddha Heart Parenting and creates a mutually respectful, enriching dynamic that is filled with clear compassionate communication from one heart to another.

Compassionate communication is used to meet our child's needs of recognition, inclusion, contribution, acceptance, consideration, and support. It is at the heart of problem solving and relationship building. When we use compassionate communication with our child from the time they are born, we seldom need to take any other action to help them to develop their own Buddha Heart of wisdom and compassion.

If we start using compassionate communication when our children are older they will most probably have developed behaviour habits that do not serve them well. We can support our child to break these habits with strategies that guide them to a deep understanding of cause and effect i.e. karma and karmic ripening. These strategies are called effect-management.

With sustained effort and sincerity
Discipline and self-control
The wise become like islands
Which no flood can overwhelm.

Dhammapada

Compassionate Communication - The Skilful Way to Communicate

Just as a mother would protect her only child at the risk of her own life,
Even so, cultivate a boundless heart towards all beings.
Let your thoughts of boundless love pervade the whole world.
Fill your mind with compassion.

Buddha.

The wise ones fashion speech with their thought,
Sifting it as grain is sifted through a sieve.

Buddha

The three chapters in this section cover compassionate communication skills and techniques. They provide an understanding of why this is the most appropriate way to communicate with our child. We are then shown how to use these skills. Compassionate communication creates a deep connection with our child.

- Compassionate Communication – What is it?

- Compassionate Communication – Identifying and Expressing Needs and Feelings

- Problem Identification & Solution-Focussed Approach

Compassionate Communication – What Is It?

There never was, there never will be,
nor is there now anyone
who is wholly blamed or wholly praised.
Dhammapada – Kodhavagga-Anger, Verse 228

This is the first of three chapters on compassionate communication. Buddha Heart Parenting is about communicating and these chapters show us how to communicate with our child and really connect. This first chapter looks at compassionate communication and why we need it. The difference between praise and feedback is discussed in detail because it is important to stop or limit praising our child and to start building their self-encouragement skills. This chapter also gives us skills we can use to do this.

The next chapter then looks at the skills of compassionate communication that allow us to look deeply into ourselves and our child and express feelings and needs. These skills are called empathic listening and self-expression. The last of the three chapters on compassionate communication gives us the skills to use a solution-focused approach to solving problems whether we have the problem or our child has the problem.

How we communicate is an important part of our Buddhist practice. Buddhism has precepts that provide a condensed form of Buddhist ethical practice, and communication features as the fourth of these precepts. This precept is about deep listening and loving speech:

Aware of suffering caused by the inability to listen to others and unmindful speech, I vow to cultivate deep listening and loving speech in order to bring joy and happiness to others and relieve others of their suffering. Knowing that words can create happiness or bring suffering, I vow to learn to speak truthfully, with words that inspire self-confidence, joy and hope.

Why is compassion important?

Buddha Heart Parenting is based on compassion – compassion for ourselves, our child and for others. Buddha Heart communication allows us to connect compassionately with ourselves and with others, and inspire compassion from them. When people know where we are coming from it tends to bring them to that place too – be it positive or negative. Compassionate communication builds compassion and is contagious. If we use compassion as the motivation for action we are more likely to engage in skilful communication and action. In this way communication is conscious and compassionate.

When we communicate compassionately we make a deep connection with others. To communicate in this way we need to develop the practice of looking deeply into ourselves, our children and others, to gain an understanding of both their feelings/emotions and needs, and our own feelings/emotions and needs. Although compassionate communication focuses on the other person, and not on ourselves, it does give recognition to our feelings/emotions and needs. This is instrumental to communication that is compassionate.

Putting the focus on the child's needs and feelings doesn't deny our feelings and needs but allows us the opportunity to be other-cherishing instead of self-cherishing. We can strike a balance with compassion for ourselves as well. It is possible to look deeply within to understand our needs and feelings and to seek to take action to have our needs met, whilst at the same time avoiding self-cherishing.

Compassionate communication recognises that behaviour comes from feelings, and emotions come from needs – either met or unmet – and if we can understand our own or our child's needs, we will understand the emotion and see their behaviour in a different light. We realise that if the needs can be met or changed, the emotion will disappear and inappropriate behaviour will cease.

Buddha Heart Parenting and communication work to change power distributions. We, as parents, often believe we have more power than our child. We feel we have the right to make them do as we say. This kind of power is 'power over'. The use of 'power over' to coerce a child to do something she doesn't want to do neither works nor builds the kind of relationship we want with our child, nor is it in the best interest of our child.

Buddha Heart Parenting moves from 'power over' to 'power with' and 'power to'. We share the 'power with' our child, and we support our child to gain the 'power to' control their own life and reach their potential. 'Power over' is a controlling approach whereas 'power with' and 'power to' together constitute an enabling or empowering approach. Which approach would Buddha take?

We all have psychological needs. The number and strength of these needs is dependent on the extent to which we have realised our own Buddha potential. Compassionate communication understands we all have needs and that our behaviour is largely determined by these needs, either met or unmet. This kind of communication attempts to meet needs and in so doing builds trusting relationships. When we engage in compassionate communication we show children how much we care.

Children don't know how much they know till they know how much we care.

Compassionate communication makes our children, whether they are babies or adolescents, feel loved and valued and when they feel this way they are:

- Happier
- Able to think for themselves
- Able to make decisions
- More optimistic
- More confident to try new things
- More responsible
- Compassionate – care about and help others
- Able to understand the Dharma

Our current communication is largely a result of habit. We develop our patterns of communication like we do other behaviour, from early socialisation and modelling. Few of us have learnt in childhood to communicate compassionately. We have not learnt to look deeply. We tend to think that communication is natural and that we are expressing ourselves naturally, but Gandhi said:

"Don't mix up that which is habitual with that which is natural."

The change we want to make will be easier if we bear this in mind. When we start changing our ineffective communication to compassionate communication this may seem unnatural to us at first and we may not feel comfortable. But it only seems this way to us because we are not used to it.

Compassionate communication guides us in reframing how we communicate. So that, instead of our communication being habitual, automatic reactions, our communication becomes a conscious response based on our findings from looking deeply within ourselves and within our child.

Using compassionate communication provides us with a valuable opportunity to practice engaged Buddhism. Right Speech is the fourth step on the Eightfold Path

Right Speech means not engaging in harsh speech, nagging, manipulating, name calling, or divisive speech. It can be easily seen that as parents we often do not engage in Right Speech with our children. When we learn and use compassionate communication we advance our Buddhist practice considerably.

When we focus on looking deeply within ourselves and within our children we will see that compassionate communication is the natural progression from looking deeply and seeing needs and feelings/emotions, to expressing or clarifying those needs and feelings/emotions. When we are aware of the needs and feelings/emotions of ourselves and our child we will want to meet those needs – again using compassionate communication. So we can see, compassionate communication is not just a skill – it is a process. It is a process that focuses our here and now awareness of feelings and needs, and then gives us actions we can take to meet those needs.

One of the greatest tools for communicating compassionately is to stop before we speak and think: What would Buddha say? This is an extremely powerful way of getting in touch with our Buddha heart.

How we view our child

Our understanding of reality determines how we communicate. We can learn all the appropriate skills but if we do not have a clear view of reality we will communicate where we are at, rather than where we want to be. That is, we will communicate ignorance instead of wisdom. For example, if our intention is still to control our child, regardless of the words we use, that is the message they will receive. Our children internalise our view of the world. Every interaction we have with our child contains messages about what life is like, who we are, and who they are.

As we work to eliminate our mental delusions and to come to understand impermanence, emptiness and the nature of conditioned reality, we will communicate from our Buddha heart of compassion. When this happens, the meeting of the intention, compassion and the appropriate words will result in a deep connection between us and our child, and true communication - compassionate communication.

A way to help us to stay centred in our Buddha heart is to consider how we view our child. Do we view the word 'child' as describing a 'less than' adult person? If we are practising equanimity, a child deserves as much respect and consideration as an adult. Would we treat our friends how we treat our child? We can treat our child as we would treat our best friend.

As mentioned earlier, one method to change our view of our child is to reflect on the possibility that she is the Buddha in a rebirth as our child. Would we treat the Buddha as we treat our child? It may be useful to see the Buddha within our child and relate to that part of her. Or, we could focus on the fact that within our child is a Buddha heart that we have an opportunity to support or help to become fully realised. Our words and actions may be very different then.

What are the skills of Compassionate Communication?

The skills of compassionate communication are developed through understanding and practice. When we have an understanding of the different kinds of communication and their consequences, along with knowing the actual skills of compassionate communication we are then able to choose the most effective communication skill for different circumstances.

All compassionate communication skills can be considered as either skills that focus on the child or skills that focus on ourselves. In any interaction we may use only one, or both, or we may alternate between one and the other. Skills that focus on the child are **feedback** (developing the skill of self-encouragement), **empathic listening**, and **problem solving** (when the child has a problem). Skills that focus on us are **self-expression**, and **solution finding** (when we have a problem).

Skills that incorporate both are **participatory decision-making, family meetings** and **joint solution finding.**

Each of these skills will be discussed starting with feedback and how to help our child to develop the skill of self-encouragement.

Skill: Giving feedback and creating self-encouragement

Whatever words we utter should be chosen with care for people will hear them and be influenced by them for good or ill.

Buddha.

What we aim to do when we praise or provide feedback is to encourage our child, to build confidence, and to support them. But there is a big difference between praise and providing feedback. It is sometimes difficult to understand this difference between praise and feedback. Let's look at praise first, and find out what it is, and then take a look at feedback and specific ways we can support self-encouragement.

What is praise?

We give a child praise whenever we make a positive evaluation or judgement. For example:

"Good boy";
"Good job;"
"Great painting";
"You did well";
"That was good work";
"What a great effort";
"I like what you did";
"I love it when you do well";
"I'm pleased you got a high mark";
"What a pretty drawing";
"You are so clever";
"Great work";

"Great effort";
"What a lovely painting".

You will notice there isn't much variation with what we say when we praise. We don't have to think very hard to praise our child. We don't have to stop what we are doing and listen to them and try to understand what they did from their perspective. When we praise we use words like 'good', 'great', 'well' etc. This simplicity is in direct contrast to feedback, which, as we shall see, has endless variations, depending on the actions of the child. Feedback requires us to stop and connect with our child before we respond.

When we say we are 'pleased', 'happy', or that we 'liked' what our child did, we are saying that what they did pleased us. The emphasis is on how we feel about what they did. They are learning how to please us. It is more beneficial to our child if the focus is on how they feel about what they did.

Praise can work counter to encouragement and often does not achieve the outcome most of us would want. Most times praise is conditional, delusional and part of conditioned reality. In contrast, feedback is reality – it is evidence-based. Feedback is verifiable by our child. Feedback provides encouragement and fosters self-encouragement. A note of caution: if our attentional bias means we focus on imperfections and errors, and our feedback focuses of these, then feedback would most likely be discouraging and negative. Our feedback needs to provide positive encouragement to our child by describing positive aspects of their behaviour.

The following features of praise refer to praise in general. There are incidents of praise that do not have some or all of these features. For example, we can say 'Wow, that is really good!' as a statement of our opinion without the negative features of praise. It is when we use praise habitually or routinely that the following features apply.

Praise is conditional. We only praise a child when they have done something we consider 'good' or 'positive' i.e. it has met some condition we set.

Praise sets up competition. When we praise one child and another doesn't get any, the second child may feel like they missed out on something and may compete to get praise. Remember praise is seen as a reward.

Praise is a judgement. We judge the behaviour as 'good' or 'right'. It is only our judgement. Another person may not judge it in the same way.

Praise seeks to control. When we offer a verbal reward i.e. praise, to our young child for putting away her toys or for drinking from a cup without spilling, who benefits? Praise has less to do with the emotional needs of our child and more to do with our convenience. Praise is just like tangible rewards (this was discussed in reward and punishment earlier). It is our way of doing something to our child to get them to do what we want. We think it will benefit them to learn these behaviours, and it will, but other ways of encouraging their behaviour are more skilful.

Praise shows children where the power base resides.
The people who praise the most are parents, teachers, and relatives and other people who are older than the child. These people often are in a position of power and this position is reinforced when they praise, since what praise is saying is: I judge that you have done something 'good' or 'right' and I will give you this verbal reward when you do it.

Praise provides external reinforcement and makes children externally-directed.
Remember when we looked at internal and external locus of control. We all want our children to rely on internal

reinforcement rather than external. Otherwise they may spend their lives looking for approval from people around them. When we praise we are giving an external reward or reinforcement that can lead to them relying on the externals to determine their sense of worth. Praise can leave a child dependent on external motivation just as much as punishment and criticism does.

Praise can raise our child to be externally rather than internally directed. We may be teaching her to make choices in life to gain the approval and acceptance of others. When our child is internally directed, i.e. has an internal locus of control, she will use her power of reason to cut through the external influences, to examine the possible consequences of the choices she can make, and she will make her decision because it is right for her and not because she thinks others will think better of her.

Buddha cautions us to foster our children's awareness that happiness and satisfaction come from inside not outside.

Praise can reduce confidence.
Research has shown that children who are praised are more hesitant and have less confidence than other children. A study that looked at the effects of praise found that children who were praised lavishly by teachers were more tentative in their responses, more apt to answer in a questioning tone of voice and tended to give up their ideas quickly if the teacher didn't seem to agree. Another effect of praise was that these children were less likely to persist with a difficult task or to share their ideas with other children.

Praise capitalises on young children's craving for our approval.
Praise works for parents because children need recognition and are very eager to gain our approval. Parents are the most important people in a child's life and it is normal for them to want to please us. This is natural. We have a responsibility not to exploit this need to our own end.

Praise can be used to manipulate.
We often manipulate children with rewards instead of using compassionate communication to help them to understand how to be compassionate in their dealings with everybody else. Praise is often used in conjunction with punishment i.e. if the child has 'good' behaviour, then the parent praises, and if the child has 'bad' behaviour, then the parent punishes. Both punishment and rewards i.e. both punishment and praise are an attempt to manipulate our child to behave how we want them to.

Praise can increase children's dependence on us.
Not all the praise we give our children is in an attempt to control them or get them to continue to behave 'well'. Sometimes we are genuinely pleased for our child and express this as praise. We want our child to have good self-esteem, but praise can make our child less secure and more dependent. The more we say 'good girl', 'good work', 'great painting', 'I like what you've done', 'I'm pleased you tidied your room', the more our child depends on us and our evaluations. They rely on our decisions about what is 'good' and 'bad' and 'right' and 'wrong'. They fail to rely on their own judgement, and they come to rely on us to determine their sense of worth. For example, if they can get us to praise them or smile at them, then they are OK.

Praise can undermine pleasure and interest.
Just as praise can undermine independence, so can it undermine pleasure and interest. Research at the University of Toronto found that young children who were frequently praised for displays of generosity tended to be slightly less generous on an everyday basis than other children were. It seems every time they heard 'Good sharing' or 'I'm so proud of you for helping', they became a little less interested in sharing or helping.

Praise can reduce the behaviour we are trying to encourage.
Praise usually does work, but only in the short term. Numerous studies have shown that children will behave 'well' or 'appropriately' when they are praised, but often this behaviour diminishes over time. Remember praise is a reward. If we have an internal locus of control, we don't like to be rewarded for our behaviour – neither do our children. We feel good when we behave appropriately simply because it feels better to contribute, cooperate, and behave with compassion. This is what we want for our children too.

Praise can de-motivate.
Children will often do something for the sheer pleasure of doing it. When they are praised for the behaviour they may loose interest in the behaviour because the joy of doing it has gone. For example, a child may love painting just for the sheer joy of putting colour on paper. Their parent says "Oh, what a good painting" and the child then looks at the painting through different eyes. They were delighting in putting colour on paper, not in producing a painting. They might not think their painting is any good at all, and therefore, rather than let the parent see that they really can't produce 'good' paintings they stop painting. The joy has gone out of the activity.

What are the alternatives?
How do we support self-encouragement?
There are several things we can do to support our child to gain the skill of self-encouragement. These alternatives below are compassionate communication in action and are used routinely in Buddha Heart Parenting.

Don't praise. This may seem self-evident given the discussion above, but we are better able to stop praising if we realise that praise can be damaging.

Please note that while many of us may have been using praise with our children, we can be encouraged to know that it is never too late to change. We are the most important people in our child's life and if we now change our responses, they can still develop an internal locus of control and all the other benefits that come from using the alternatives to praise.

Say nothing. This is a valuable skill in compassionate communication. To say nothing can say a lot. Saying nothing in some situations will communicate to our child that they are doing fine, are in control, and we have faith and confidence in them and their abilities. We can realise that our child doesn't need rewards to behave well. We can let her discover that appropriate behaviour has its own rewards.

Provide feedback. We can report what we saw. This is sometimes called evidence-based feedback. It is verifiable by our child. We say what we saw eg

"You put the last block on without it falling over."
"The ball went through the net."

This feedback process can focus on the feelings of the child, by using empathic listening eg

"You look really pleased with yourself?" "You sound happy about getting an invitation?"

This skill will be discussed later. We can also provide feedback about how their actions and words have affected us. This is self-expression and we will discuss this skill in the next chapter.

Ask for more information. When we ask for information about an achievement or something our child has done or is doing, we help them to connect with what they like, or feel positive, about what they did, eg

"Tell me about your picture?"
"What was the hardest part of this project?"

What we are trying to do is to get the child to identify what they have done or what external circumstances were making it difficult for them. If they can phrase answers in their own words they learn to encourage themselves. When they put it in their own language they can better own it. Asking for information also shows our child that we are trying to connect with them and understand their feelings.

Call attention to others reactions, We can help our child to connect with how their actions have benefited others eg

"Did you see how pleased Jane seemed when you shared your toy?"
"I noticed Sean stopped crying when you supported him."

We can also draw attention to how their actions or words benefited us eg

"That made it easier for me."
"When we do things together I have fun."
"I enjoyed that story you read – I can visualise the story better when I hear the words."

Children have a need to contribute and cooperate and this kind of communication helps them to see how they have achieved this.

Use compassionate communication. When we use compassionate communication whenever we talk with our child she is able to live without judgement and blame. She is then able to experience doing things from her own internal motivation and is therefore more satisfied.

Use positive presuppositions. A presupposition is something that supposes that it is true, at least in part. A presupposition can be either positive or negative. Most presuppositions we use are negative and de-motivate, and discourage appropriate behaviour and effort. Positive presuppositions, on the other hand, encourage our child and build the confidence to act, and build belief in themselves.

The following are examples of **negative** presuppositions:

"What have you done this time?" – the supposition is that they are always doing something 'wrong'.
"What else could you add to the picture?" – the supposition is that the picture is incomplete.
"See, you can behave when you try." – the supposition is that they don't try to behave.
"I like what you've done, but you need to improve." – the supposition is that the child hasn't done well, They haven't lived up to our standards.

The following are examples of **positive** presuppositions:

"How pleased are you with this?" – the supposition is that their work has given them pleasure and satisfaction.
"When I've finished this I'll listen to your story." – the supposition is that you are keen to hear their story.
"Do you want to put this away before or after lunch?" – the supposition is that they will put it away – the question is only about when.
"I wonder who will ask the first question?" – the supposition is that someone will ask a question.
"Can you tell me how soon you will finish this?" – the supposition is that it will be finished.

Presuppositions alter or reinforce our frames of reference. When we have more than one frame of reference, we can choose which one is more appropriate. The use of positive presuppositions helps our child to reframe what they believe about themselves. It helps to develop self-encouragement skills.

Provide an example. We help our child to be internally directed and to use self-encouragement by our example. We provide the model for many of the blueprints for our child's sense of self. When we rely on external rewards or praise to feel worthwhile, the message we are transmitting to our children is that we all need others to determine how we feel about ourselves. Is this the message we want to give to our children.

We need to give our children a positive example. Once we start to think about it we probably notice just how conditioned we are to external rewards. We try hard to get the 'right' job (external), buy a house in the 'right' suburb (external), and wear the 'right' clothes (dictated by the fashion industry), and mix with the 'right' people (external). We work hard in a job we don't necessarily like, to have the reward of the paypacket (external reward) that lets us buy things that have been defined by the media and our social group as 'cool' (externally determined), so that we will have some popularity in the social setting (externally determined). Not only are our children astute enough to see what is happening, they hear us talking about how we have 'failed' when we fail to achieve these things.

If we want our children to adopt an internal frame of reference and to use self-encouragement we will make it easier for them if we change how we view the world. This is where Buddhism can help us by gaining an understanding of concepts such as impermanence and attachment. As we examine the different areas of our life we can to ask ourselves "Are we making this choice because it is 'right' for us or because it is a means of gaining the approval and love of the outside world?" I am a firm believer that children learn from knowing what is happening in our head on issues such as these. As we go through the internal dialogue of examining why we make the choices we make, we can make this dialogue external by talking it through out loud. This process of pondering, weighing and considering, helps our children to develop their own positive self-talk.

Once we have changed, our children have a better chance of setting internal systems that determine their self worth. Although children can pick up these beneficial internal frames of reference without us expressing our internal dialogue aloud, we can talk about how we feel when we do things eg

*"I feel really good that I helped Susan with her move –
She really needed the support."*
*"I like what I have done in the garden, I think it looks
very effective."*
*"When I saw the smile on Jason's face when he saw
what I'd done, I felt I had made a real contribution."*

What is shaping?

Shaping is a strategy we can use to help our child learn a
complicated task or a task they are having difficulty with. What
we do is break the task down into smaller tasks and provide
feedback as the child masters each one. For example, tasks such
as tying shoelaces can be taught by shaping. Rather than
waiting for the child to learn to tie their shoelaces before
encouraging them and sharing their pleasure that they have
succeeded, we can break down the procedure into small stages
and comment on each partial skill they achieve such as making
the first knot. Then we can encourage their achievement at
making the loops etc.

Another example of shaping that involves an older child is
supporting them to learn to shoot hoops with a basketball. We
can encourage our child as they develop more control of the
ball, as they are able to get sufficient height, when they can
bounce the ball off the backboard, shooting on the run etc.

These alternatives to praise avoid instilling the belief in our
children that they need people and things in the outside world
to bolster their self-worth. To further support them in this and
in the development of compassion and other-cherishing we can
give love or kindness to others without expecting anything in
return. Few people do things without thought of getting
something in return. When we have expectations of
reciprocity, we develop an attitude of entitlement or self-
cherishing. Some of us might disagree with this statement but
if we look deeply we are likely to find that almost everything
we do, we do to get something back. The 'something back' may
only be recognition that we did something 'nice', but most of
us do expect something in return.

Saying 'thank you' can have negative effects

If we always expect a 'thank you' for our acts of kindness, we are expecting to get something back for what we give out. We feel that we are entitled to this by the rules of our society, and when we don't get it we may think the other person is rude. This is a judgement based on our sense of entitlement. There are many cultures where there is no word for thank you because these cultures acknowledge that when we give to another we have reward enough in just doing that, we do not need the reward of 'thank you'. Our aim is only to help them.

In our Western culture where many of us don't want the feeling of being beholden or obligated, we may say 'thank you' too often. By saying 'thank you' we give back to the person who gave us something and so the favour slate is clean. Try not saying 'thank you' next time someone gives you something. The act of giving is somehow amplified when we don't say 'thank you'. A mere 'thank you' can be a thoughtless (without real thought) act and when we flesh out the benefit the gift has brought us, we make a better connection with the giver of the gift.

If we do things for other people without the expectation of anything in return we would do things anonymously more often and we would not want, and indeed may feel uncomfortable with a 'thank you'.

When we do something for others we feel 'good' inside. This feeling is the best motivator. But for many of us it isn't what motivates us, or it isn't enough by itself to motivate us. How many times have we heard someone say something like:

"I'm always doing things for her, and she never even thanks me. I'm not going to help her anymore!"

So what do we say when someone does something for us or gives us something? The thing that amplifies their joy in giving is for them to see or hear how and why, what they did has changed our situation. For example:

"Oh, that meal you sent over yesterday made such as difference to things at home. It gave me the time to look after Petra who was very sick."

or:

"What you said has given me the courage to stand up for myself."

or:

"I have wanted to read this book for ages, but haven't had the money to buy it."

When is it appropriate to give our opinion?

I have said that praise gives an evaluation and judgement, and that this is external reinforcement that is not beneficial to our child. This does not mean that we can never give an evaluation. There are times when it is appropriate for us to give an evaluation. Just sometimes our child may genuinely want our opinion on what they have done, or on how to make something 'better'. This is fine. She may need some feedback that gives an evaluation to know how to do something differently or how to improve something. This is fine. It is not beneficial when the child looks to us to determine her self worth.

These alternatives to praise outlined here do not need to be memorised as a new script. When we keep in mind our long-term goals for our children, are mindful of where we are coming from, and what may be the effects of what we say, we will find it easy to adopt the alternatives to praise.

Compassionate Communication - Identifying and Expressing Needs and Feelings

See yourself in others
Then whom can you hurt?
What harm can you do?

Buddha

This chapter will give us the skills to look deeply within ourself and within our child to identify needs and feelings/emotions, and then to express those needs and feelings/emotions. These are powerful skills that allow both parents and children to see objectively, and so enter solution-finding quickly. When we use these skills we are amazed at how quickly inappropriate behaviour disappears. Which also means that inappropriate behaviour no longer bothers us – emotions of annoyance, anger, etc will disappear because instead of just reacting, we will be able to quickly cut to seeing needs. We are then able to find the most beneficial way to have everyone's needs met.

There are two key skills in compassionate communication that allow us to do this. We use empathic listening when we are trying to identify our child's feelings/emotions and needs, and we use self-expression when we are expressing our own feelings/emotions and needs.

Empathic listening and self-expression often form a dialogue with sometimes one being more appropriate, and sometimes the other. There is a simple rule for determining which of the two compassionate communication skills to use. If the child has the problem, use empathic listening. If we have the problem, start with self-expression. When we both have the problem start with empathic listening.

What is Empathic Listening

It has been said that 90 percent of inappropriate behaviour comes from children wanting adults to listen to them. We know we feel better when we feel heard and understood. Often it is more important to feel understood than to get what we thought we wanted. It is the same for children. For example, children may kick up a fuss because they didn't get an object another child did. When we empathically listen to their feeling and need for recognition they are happy – even though they still didn't get the object the other child has.

We need skills in empathic listening so our children feel understood and we need skills in self-expression so our children will understand us.

Empathic listening is listening with our heart.

Many people think that empathy and sympathy are synonyms, but this is not the case. Empathy is the power of projecting one's mind and heart into the object of contemplation i.e. our child or the other person, to understand their feelings and thoughts. Sympathy is a feeling or an expression of pity or sorrow for the distress of another. We can see that empathy, in contrast to sympathy, is an identification with, and understanding of, another's situation, feelings and motives.

If we are empathic of another person's situation we can be sympathetic as well, and if we are sympathetic we may be empathetic. But experiencing one does not mean we will experience the other.

Put simply, empathy is to **feel** the emotion, sympathy is to feel **for** the emotion. For example a con person may possess, and actually rely on having, empathy i.e. awareness of others' thoughts and feelings, but may fail to experience sympathy. Having empathy allows her the means to extort from others. If she felt sympathy she would not extort from others and cause them suffering.

It is more difficult to be empathic than to be sympathetic.

Empathic listening is sometimes called reflective listening. Empathic listening lies on a continuum of listening, which goes from ignoring what someone is saying, to pretending to listen, to selective listening, to active listening, to empathic listening.

Empathic listening involves full listening – we listen with our eyes, ears, brain, and heart. It involves experiencing, really experiencing, another person's frame of reference or worldview. When we use this skill we have an attitude of curiosity, grace, compassion, and peace. Empathic listening brings together the qualities of a child, Mother Theresa and the Dalai Lama. We attempt to listen from our Buddha Heart, being totally present in the moment, and we try to focus, and to have a real desire to understand the other person, their words, their feelings and emotions, their needs, and their worldview.

Empathic listening is an opportunity for change and transformation, not just for transfer of information. When we listen empathically we allow the person to move beyond their feelings and emotions to find solutions. Emotions are generated in the right hemisphere of the brain. While emotions run high, this side of the brain is dominant. The person cannot easily switch to the left hemisphere where logical, rational, problem-solving thought is found.

If we want to support, or influence our child, we have first to understand them. This allows them to move from the right hemisphere to the left, and it is when this happens they are able to listen and understand us.

There is a story of a professor who went to a Zen monk to find out how to become enlightened. The professor talked on and on about his philosophies and theories. The monk interrupted to ask the professor if he would like a drink of tea.

The professor said 'yes' and then continued to talk about his theories. The monk filled the professors cup and continued to pour. The cup began to overflow. After a few minutes the professor noticed the monk was still pouring and the tea was running all over the table and floor. In agitation the professor said: "What are you doing? Can't you see the cup is full?" The monk smiled calmly and said: "Yes, I can. This cup is like your mind. Your mind is so full of its own ideas there is no room in it for you to hear anything I might have to teach you."

We need to listen to our children as a deer listens to sounds

If we want to be understood, we have first to understand. This is why the focus is put on empathic listening. We cannot help another unless we first understand them. By hearing the feelings and needs beneath our child's words and behaviours, we offer them precious gifts. We have the opportunity to help them understand, express, and find ways to meet their needs. We also model ways to empathise with others – another precious gift to give our child.

Inappropriate habitual ways of responding to our child's feelings

We have habitual ways of communicating and sometimes these ways are not beneficial to either ourselves or to the other person. When someone else talks we often listen 'with an intention to reply' – not 'with an intention to understand'. When someone has painful feelings, we have a tendency to:

Fix: advise, lecture, moralise, reassure;
Evaluate: judge, generalise, disagree, analyse;
Interpret: story tell, advise;
Probe: question, interrogate;
Vent: blame, defend, disagree.

Below are some of our habitual responses that are inappropriate for empathic listening:

"What you should do is..."
"If I were you, I'd..."
"I would have helped but..."
"That's not true..."
"But you're the one who..."
"Oh, you poor thing..."
"How can people do that..."
"I know how you feel..."
"It could've been a lot worse..."
"You did the best you could..."
"How come you did that..."
"You're just too unrealistic.."
"The trouble with them is.."
"That's nothing. Listen to this.."

These responses often seem to come naturally to us, but they are far from natural. They are learned responses and they meet needs of ours not the other person's. Our need may be to feel important, good, or virtuous. Our need may be to avoid their pain, or to avoid feeling their situation. We want their painful emotions to just go away – and the quicker the better. We may think we want their suffering to end because we feel compassion for them and don't want them to suffer. But many times, we want their suffering, or their expression of suffering, to end so we don't suffer also.

How do we listen empathically?

The aim of empathic listening is to understand our child's needs and feelings or emotions, and in so doing develop a heartfelt connection with her. The first step in empathic listening is to **enter our Buddha heart** and feel compassion for our child.

The next step occurs naturally if we feel compassion – we will **temporarily put aside our opinions, needs and emotions**. If this does not occur easily we can remind ourselves that we cannot influence our child and his decisions until he feels understood. If we want to be understood, first we need to seek to understand.

Be mindfully in the present moment. We can make the choice to be mindful of our child. We can focus solely and non-judgmentally on him. This means we try to not just focus on his words, but on the whole of him. We can look for body language – watch his face, eyes, body, and hands – and note his postures, movements, expressions and gestures or lack of these. We can also listen for other verbal aspects such as tone, volume, and hesitancy.

Guesstimate our child's current thoughts, feelings, emotions, and needs. It is important to remember we won't know what our children are thinking or feeling or what needs they have unless they tell us directly, or until they confirm our guesstimation. We often think we know what is inside another person, but only that person knows – until they share this with us. And when they share their feelings, we have to realise that this information is accurate only for that moment. It may be different in the next moment. Emotions can change once we have talked about them, but needs are more enduring. Needs, met or unmet, determine our feelings and emotions, and one of our child's needs is to feel understood. When we are understood we can then focus on our other needs more objectively. This is also true for our children.

Check the timing. Timing is everything. We have a tendency to jump in too soon. We don't listen enough. We want to help our child, so we jump to the next steps of reflecting and rephrasing too soon. As a general rule, we go to problem solving much too soon. If we find we are tempted to jump to the next step too soon, we can focus on our child's needs and emotions again, and reaffirm the importance of this step. We need to use wisdom with compassion to know what to do and when to do it, or if to act at all.

Rephrase the content and reflect the feeling. We need to check what we think they are saying and feeling, is indeed what they are saying and feeling. We can check the *content* of the message by putting the message into our own words. For example

They might say: *"I have a problem."*

We could rephrase as: *"Something's wrong?"*

This may seem strange and unnatural at first, but children need to know that we are trying to understand. It also helps our child see the situation more clearly. We can check what our child is *feeling* by reflecting what we think the child might be feeling. For example

Our child might say: *"I don't want to do this anymore."*

And we might say: *"Sounds like you are feeling discouraged"*.

This reflection uses the right hemisphere of the brain because we are mirroring the emotion or feeling that is involved in the message.

Rather than just rephrasing separately, what our child said, and what he is feeling, the more effective skill is to be able to do both things together. This involves both hemispheres of the brain together – the left checks what was said, and the right picks up the feeling.

For example, when our child said *"I don't want to do this anymore,"* we could pick up both the content and feeling and reply: *"Sounds like you are feeling discouraged because you aren't getting the results you were expecting."*

It is important with empathic listening to set the tone as a guesstimate not as a statement where we are telling the child how they feel. We can do this by giving our response with an inflection at the end, connoting a question. We can also do this by using opening phrases like the following:

"Seems you're unsure of..."
"It sounds like..."
"It seemed to you that...."
"So you think that...."
"You're anxious about...."
"I get the impression..."
"Your frown seems to say..."
"Looks as if....."
"I guess what you'd like is...."

This skill is much more difficult than the two separate skills and it is the most valuable part of empathic listening. We may need to practice, practice, practice. We can practice in our everyday life with all the people we come into contact with.

Problems and Pitfalls to effective empathic listening

We need to be vigilant in the early stages of learning compassionate communication skills to make sure we don't revert to old patterns of communication or old attitudes. We also need to be aware that things will not always go to plan when we use empathic listening. Below are some of the problems or barriers we may encounter and some of the pitfalls to avoid.

When we first start compassionate communication we find we **don't have a very large emotion vocabulary**. We know angry, annoyed, hurt, happy, but what about all the other emotion words? There is a list of emotion words at the end of the book to help build an emotion vocabulary. With practice we will find we can quickly identify a word to fit the emotion. Using a range of emotion words helps develop our child's emotion vocabulary too.

Our old patterning is strong and we will feel drawn to 'help' the other person. Here is an effective analogy to show the effects of our old style versus the effects of empathic listening.

Imagine putting a knife blade into a stream of running water. Imagine putting the blade in the same direction as the flow of water. See what happens? The water keeps flowing with almost no change. This is similar to empathic listening. Now imagine putting the knife blade at right angles to the flow of water. What happens? The water hits the blade and splashes up before trying to continue downwards. The water is disrupted.

This same disruption happens in the communication process when we put in our opinions, needs, or thoughts. If we feel a need to do this it is a good indication we have entered a self-cherishing headspace. When we commit to be a listener we are being entrusted with someone's vulnerability, we need to stay centred on them. If we feel the desire to put in our thoughts, opinions, or needs it is time to be mindful, and re-enter our Buddha heart before continuing.

We can overuse empathic listening. We will find that empathic listening works really well and we want to use it all the time. This is a pitfall. We can use empathic listening too much, turning every conversation into a deep therapeutic session. We all know the feeling when we come across someone who does this. We can save these skills for when another person needs their emotions, feelings and needs to be understood.

When our child is talking about her problem **we may feel we need to be saying more** to show that we are interested. Our interest is shown in our body language and it is picked up from our intention.

When we use empathic listening we are freeing our child to talk about their problem/s. **It may take quite some time.** Unless we have the time right then to listen and problem solve with our child it is best not to use empathic listening. If we think our child has a problem, we can say:

> *"It looks like things didn't go well today. I would really love to hear about it. I have to go out now, so how about we talk when I get home."*

Make sure, if we say we will talk later, that we do talk later.

When we use empathic listening **it may appear to us that our child feels more pain** than he did before we started. When we listen empathically our child will be able to get in touch with their emotions better, and this may appear to exacerbate the emotions, but it doesn't. The more children can get in touch with their emotions and their needs the more they will be in a better position to release their emotions and move to finding solutions.

There is no right response in empathic listening. Since we are guesstimating what our child is feeling, it doesn't matter if we are wrong. They will put us right. The important thing is that we are genuinely trying to understand.

Empathic listening is listening with our heart. It is as easy as that.

What is self-expression?

Self-expression refers to how we communicate our needs and emotions to others. In all our communication with others we need to be respectful. This is especially important when we are expressing our needs and emotions.

For many of us when dealing with our child's inappropriate behaviour, our usual tendency is to blame, reprimand, remind, offer incentives or punish. This style of communication doesn't lead to our child developing an internal locus of control or to them developing compassion.

Focussing on needs shifts the attention away from judgements about our children's and our own behaviour and actions. When we focus on needs we are able to see the specific behaviours and conditions that are affecting us, without the emotive judgement and blame. We also learn to express clearly exactly what we would like to be happening in any given situation.

When we focus on needs and use empathic listening and self-expression to communicate we are learning to consider both our own needs and the needs of our child. We then see that it is not beneficial to give in to our child's every wish. When we model consideration of everyone's needs, not just the child's, we are providing our child with a model of a way of living where power is shared.

The skills in self-expression guide us in reframing how we express ourselves, so that instead of being habitual, automatic reactions, our communication becomes conscious responses that follow from looking deeply into ourselves, and that simultaneously respect others and their needs and feelings.

The actual skill or process of self-expression is not complicated but it is powerfully transformative. Using these skills we are able to separate the dross from reality, and our relationship with our child becomes enriched from the deeper connection that results.

How do we use self-expression?

Three, five, three: Self-expression involves taking **three** steps before we actually express ourselves/talk. The actual wording of our response has **five** components, and there are **three** levels of self-expression depending on the situation. There is something in the old adage to count to three.

The first three steps: In preparation for speech we need to stop and do three things.

The first thing to do is to **observe** what is happening. This involves just looking at what is happening. Looking without evaluation or judgement.

Next we **look deeply** to see what need of ours is either not being met, or is being met, not being met, or being met, by what is happening. It helps at this stage, to observe what is happening again because sometimes our emotions are too strong to allow us to just observe what we see or hear, or in what we **think** we see or hear.

Finally we need to **connect** with our Buddha heart so that we will speak with compassion and respect.

These preparatory activities will become second nature in time, but when we first begin to use self-expression we may find it helpful to use these activities as a checklist and consciously do each one. As we develop our Buddha mind and gain a deeper understanding of karma, the mental poisons, and impermanence, we will find these steps easier and they will soon become automatic. This is why the practice of Buddhism and Buddha Heart Parenting go hand in hand. To learn the skills without the deep connection to our Buddha heart will not result in the outcomes that are beneficial for our child and for ourselves.

The five components of self-expression:

1. Describing what happened;
2. Outlining how these events affect us or others;
3. Mentioning how we feel,
4. Expressing our need, and
5. Clearly stating what we would like to happen.

It is important not only that we understand these five components, but also that we are able to put each component into words without blame, judgement or the use of manipulative language or intention.

1 – Describe what happened or is happening i.e. the behaviour. Try to just describe, don't blame, or judge – be objective. This seems simple to do but if we watch our words often we will find we are not just describing what happened. Examples of describing what happened:

> "The food is falling off the plate onto the tablecloth."
> "The bike is leaving marks on the carpet."
> "The noise of the TV is really loud."
> "The stamps are falling out of granddad's stamp album."

2 – **Outline how the behaviour affects us.** We can make this concrete and tangible, rather than vague. It is important that the other person understands how their behaviour affects us otherwise they will not see any reason to change or modify what they are doing. We can extend the examples given above:

> *"The food is falling off the plate onto the tablecloth. It is difficult for me to get it clean."*
> *"The bike is leaving marks on the carpet and it will cost a lot to have someone clean it"*
> *"The noise of the TV is really loud. I am having trouble hearing on the phone"*
> *"The stamps are falling out of granddad's stamp album. Granddad won't be able to replace some of those stamps if they get lost"*

3 – **Mention how we feel** as a result of the effect of the behaviour. We can check to make sure we are expressing an emotion not a thought or an analysis. If we start to say "I feel like you..." – this is not a feeling, it is a judgement. Or "I think that..." – this is not a feeling, it is a belief.

At first it may be difficult to identify the emotion. We are very familiar with *upset, angry, annoyed, mad, etc,* but most of the time when we think we feel these emotions we are actually feeling some other emotion, but don't have a word for it. A bigger emotion vocabulary would make it easier to identify this underlying emotion. Look at the list of emotions at the end of the book to get an idea of the range of possible emotions. Many people find it useful to copy this list and put it in a prominent place in their home eg on the wall or beside the mirror or on the refrigerator, until they have increased their emotion vocabulary. The greater our repertoire of emotion words the more emotion literate our child will be too.

Here are some examples of how to mention how we feel as a result of the effect of the behaviour. These examples build on the previous examples:

"The food is falling off the plate onto the tablecloth. And I feel concerned because it is difficult for me to get it clean."

"The bike is leaving marks on the carpet. I feel anxious because I don't have any spare money and it will cost me a lot to have someone clean it"

"The noise of the TV is really loud. I'm feeling frustrated because I'm having trouble hearing on the phone"

"The stamps are falling out of granddad's stamp album. I'm worried that granddad won't be able to replace some of those stamps he has taken so long to collect, if they get lost"

Before we look at the last two components of self-expression let's look at the emotion we hear about most – anger.

What is anger?

Many people believe anger is a primary emotion and that it is legitimate to feel and express anger. Others believe anger is a secondary emotion. I tend to agree with this latter view. We feel anger when we want to change the external environment. What we feel first is any one of a number of emotions such as annoyed, hurt, frustrated, rejected. Imagine we are talking to someone and they aren't listening. What we are talking about is important to us. We want the other person to understand our point of view. We feel frustrated because we aren't getting our message across. We are feeling disrespected because the other person isn't bothering to listen. These emotions build and we become increasingly uncomfortable. We want to change the situation. We want them to listen to us. We want to lash out and make them listen. We think we feel angry now. We probably weren't even aware we were feeling frustrated or disrespected, we only notice when we feel like doing something to change the situation. We use anger to attempt to change the external environment to get rid of our primary emotions – in this case frustrated and disrespected.

In this situation, acknowledging our emotions of frustration and disrespect puts us in touch with our needs i.e. to be listened to and to be treated with respect. As soon as we can acknowledge our true emotions and needs we are already moving into solution mode rather than confrontation mode.

So, every time we catch ourself thinking we are angry, or upset, we can stop and look deeply inside to identify what we are really feeling beneath the anger.

Personal responsibility for our emotions and thoughts

Buddhism helps us to understand that we create our own emotions and thoughts – not someone else. We have to accept responsibility for what we feel – we have created those emotions with our mind. Sometimes we have developed such a strong pattern of emotions that we believe we are right to blame others for how we feel. After all, if they hadn't done ... we wouldn't feel ...

Young children can often be heard saying "He made me angry" and "She made me sad". These children are saying what they have heard others say. Often these children grow up and as adults will still say "He made me angry". This is unskilful thinking. What happens outside us does not determine what happens on the inside. What happens on the inside determines how we interpret and respond to the outside environment.

We are 100 percent responsible for how we feel and what we think. We are responsible for situations that happen *to* us because of the law of karma. We have sown karmic seeds in the past by our thoughts, words and actions, and we can provide the right conditions for these karmic seeds to ripen. By changing our thoughts, words and actions in the present moment we can prevent past karmic seeds from ripening. This applies to either positive or negative effects of past actions. In this way we are responsible for, and able to control, everything that we experience. This is a very positive realisation. We can create the kind of future we want by our thoughts and actions today.

Karma creates all, like an artist.
Karma composes, like a dancer.

Buddha

Once we accept full responsibility for how we react to the external environment we will no longer blame, judge, accuse, argue, demand etc. The brain is a pattern making organ and the longer our history of blaming, judging, accusing, arguing, demanding the stronger the pattern. We have to retrain our brain and create new patterns – patterns that benefit both ourselves and those around us.

If we can see that we are responsible for our own emotions and that they result from a faulty view of the world we often will be much more objective in looking at our children's behaviour. This objectivity has no emotion but allows us to see what is happening and to communicate compassionately using either self-expression or empathic listening, or both depending on the needs of the situation.

So, looking deeply allows us to see through our Buddha heart. Doing this we can see beyond our inappropriate patterning and identify our emotions and needs. When we identify emotions like abandoned, abused, attacked, rejected, disrespected, manipulated or unsupported, we have clues to our need that is unmet. For example, if we feel rejected, we have a need to feel accepted.

Now lets get back to the last two components of self-expression.

4 – Express our need. Our emotions arise from our needs. Depending on the extent to which we have actualised our Buddha heart, we need some or all of the following; recognition, inclusion, autonomy, influence, cooperation, contribution, belonging, generosity, achievement, acceptance, order, social contact, status, understanding, support, safety, connection, empathy, love, peace, and reassurance. When we identify our need we can express this with respect. It is often beneficial to connect the emotion to the need eg

"I feel frustrated because I need to contribute."
or
"I feel sad because I need respect".

Note the difference between "I need respect" and "I need you to be polite to me". When we express our needs it is more effective to express them universally rather than personally. That is, take the 'you' out of what we say.

The greatest risk of miscommunication lies in expressing our emotions and our needs. We are patterned beings and our minds are often patterned from childhood to manipulate, blame, judge, defend etc.

5 - Clearly ask for the change we want. In some situations we expect the other person or our child to be a mind reader. We think that if we tell them how their behaviour is affecting us they will know what we want them to do. Even though it may seem obvious to us, sometimes we have to be explicit in requesting the other person to modify their behaviour.

When we voice an explicit request, we can focus on making sure that we express our request in a way that is not taken by our child to be a demand. We have a right to express our need and to request a change in behaviour but not a right to make the child change, unless their behaviour puts someone at risk of injury.

If we are using self-expression merely as a prelude to making our child modify or cease their behaviour, then our intention is to manipulate and force our child to change. This is not compassionate communication and if we do this we are not coming from our Buddha heart.

Children are expert at picking up the intention behind our words, and responding or reacting to this intention. When they think we are going to blame or punish them if they don't modify or stop their behaviour, they will resist us. We will not make the connection to our child that we want, and our child will lose an opportunity to learn compassion.

Some times we may think we are only requesting but if our child refuses to change, we get angry and insist. This tells us that our motivation was to **make** the child change. If our motivation was pure, then when our child resisted us, we would be able to respond with empathic listening to attempt to understand their need. From this position we could become solution-focussed to identify a win-win solution.

In making a specific request we need to avoid being vague eg "Please be respectful". A child rightly would have difficulty knowing what we wanted them to do or not do. Our message would be clearer if we said:

"Would you be willing to talk with me quietly?"

It also helps to phrase our request positively rather than negatively eg

"Would you throw the ball outside?" instead of "Don't throw the ball in the house."

Putting it all together.

In putting the five components of self-expression together we need to consider the second set of three levels, i.e. the three levels of self-expression. This will determine just which components we use in any situation.

The second three levels. If we went around using all five components of self-expression all the time, nobody would listen to us. It would become monotonous and sound like we were self-cherishing and manipulative.

We use either one, two, three, four or five of the components depending on the situation and the history. We may start out in a situation using just one or two components of self-expression, and depending on our child's response we may decide to add more components to help our child to understand our needs more clearly. Or we may stop at one or two components and use empathic listening to understand what needs the child has that would be restricted if our need was met.

Most times it is enough to describe the behaviour, or maybe to describe the behaviour and its effects on us or others. To include what we would like to happen or how we feel is seldom needed. Often children are unaware of what they are doing within the bigger picture – they may be so engrossed.

For instance, our children started out sitting in the lounge playing quietly. As they play they become progressively louder. We are watching TV and the noise level becomes high enough to make it difficult for us to hear.

If we just mention "the noise is loud", **(component 1)** they might realise they are noisy and quieten down.

We could let them know that "the noise is making it difficult for me to hear the TV" **(components 1&2)**. Children, just like the rest of us, will usually modify their behaviour when they realise it is inconveniencing someone else. They have a need to cooperate and contribute.

If they don't quieten down we could tell them how we feel and what our need is eg "I feel distracted and need to be able to hear the TV" **(components 3&4)**.

We could also let them know what we would like to happen eg "would you be willing to play more quietly or play somewhere else?"**(component 5)**.

Here is another example. If my child is in the habit of leaving her toys on the floor and I often trip on them when we go to the kitchen for a drink of water during the night, I might only need to say "When toys are left on the floor at night, I trip on them when I go to the kitchen." Most children, and in fact most people, would reply "Oh, I didn't realise. I'll make sure I put them away before I go to bed." They may say nothing but mentally note that they will put them away. For something like this, we could say no more, assuming our child is responsible and caring and will put them away. This is a positive expectation and shows our belief in our child.

If the toys are not put away that night, then the next morning we could go to the next level and say "When the toys are left on the floor at night, I am concerned that I may trip and hurt myself when I go to the kitchen." We would expect a reply from this self-expression. If none comes, then we could go to the next level and clearly state our request "Would you be willing to pick them up before you go to bed?" This leaves our child in no doubt as to the behaviour, the effects for us, how we feel about it, and exactly what we would like them to do.

We need to remember, we are only expressing ourself respectfully – we are not demanding that they will change their behaviour. If self-expression doesn't give us a solution to our problem then we could adopt a solution-focused approach, either by ourself or with our child. Solution-finding and the solution-focussed approach are the topic of the next chapter.

Difficulties in using self-expression

1. It can be difficult to change. One of the biggest difficulties in using self-expression is in undoing the inappropriate patterned responses from our past. Our tendencies to blame, judge etc need to be overcome and we need to find new ways to express ourselves. This is where our study and practice of Buddhism works in combination with skill development. Buddhism helps us to develop our Buddha heart so we are coming from a position based on compassion and wisdom. Skill development gives the language and behaviour that support our new position. Together, they become Buddha Heart Parenting and support us and our child in furthering spiritual progress.

We may need to reframe our communication, and learn new ways of communicating that reflect our new position of taking responsibility for our thoughts and emotions. When we don't take responsibility we tend to use 'you' statements. Below are some examples of inappropriate 'you' communications and some possible compassionate alternatives.

Note in the last example that the alternative was to use empathic listening. When we encounter opposition from our child it is often because their needs are not being met. We need to use the compassionate communication skill of empathic listening to understand their needs in this case before we use self-expression to express our needs and emotions. Remember to be other-cherishing and understand their needs before helping them to see our needs. This doesn't mean their needs are more important but it gives recognition to the fact that they will not hear us until they feel heard – if we want to be understood, first we need to seek to understand.

Also we may notice that many of the 'you' statements are coming from a position of power, control and manipulation. When we use these statements we are trying to exert control by

'You' statements	Responsible alternatives
Judging: "You are so inconsiderate" "You are lazy." "Can't you see the dog needs to go outside. You are so irresponsible."	"I feel disrespected when I am ignored" "I feel rushed when I have to do all the cleaning up." "I see the dog needs to go outside."
Accusing: "You make me so angry" "You've made me late." "You broke your promise."	"I have chosen to let it bother me when ....." "I'll be late now." "I felt let down."
Ordering/Demanding: "Pick up your things, now."	"When things are left on the floor, it looks cluttered and I feel embarrassed when we have visitors."
Moralising: "You should ...."	"Would you be willing to ... ."

Moralising: *"You should ...."*	*"Would you be willing to ... ."*
Threatening: *"If you don't pick them up now, I'll ...."*	*"When things are left all over the house, I feel embarrassed because ..... ."*
Sarcastic: *"You haven't put the rubbish out all day. What are you waiting for, a written invitation?"* *"Of course, you know everything don't you."*	*"The rubbish needs to be taken out."* *"Sounds like you think I am being unreasonable?"*

intimidation or put-downs to the other person. This style of communication will most probably provoke defensive and/or hostile reactions from our child. When we come from our Buddha heart we could not use this style of communication. Could you imagine the Buddha saying any of these things?

2. Overuse. Self-expression is very powerful because we all have a need to cooperate and contribute. Sometimes parents overuse self-expression because it gets such good results. This may be an indication that the parent wants to have all their needs met without consideration of their child's needs. When we overuse self-expression our child and others will become tired of hearing all about how their behaviour affects us and how we feel. This is understandable – its overuse comes from a self-cherishing position.

We need to learn to discern those situations where self-expression is appropriate and where it is not. As we develop our understanding of why our children behave inappropriately, and as we start to solve some problems without including our children, we will find we use self-expression less. Also as we seek to understand Buddhist principles more we will find a balance in our communication with others.

3. Self-expression is not just in the words. Sometimes we forget that self-expression is just that - a respectful expression of what we feel and what our needs are. Because we may not have as yet internalised the basis of compassionate communication we use self-expression in the same way we have used 'you' statements in the past – to control, intimidate, blame etc. We need to understand our personal responsibility for what we think and feel. When we come from this base we will not misuse self-expression.

Our children will pick up our intention and the motivation that lies behind our words. Remember 70 percent of communication is non-verbal. That is, we communicate with tone of voice, volume of speech, and intonation, body position, facial expression (body language); and many other subtle messages that are not to be found in the actual words.

If our intention and motivation is not coming from our Buddha heart, it is hard enough to 'get the words right' let alone control all the non-verbal communication signals we are transmitting.

4. Children can feel responsible for our feelings. We want our children to gain an internal locus of control and to act skilfully and appropriately because that gives them pleasure rather than because of how we feel about their actions. When we include more components than is necessary in our self-expression, our children may become too strongly tuned to how their behaviour is affecting us and our emotional state. This can make our children feel responsible for our state of mind and give her the impression that she has the power to control how we feel. This situation would not usually occur between adults, but because children feel their parents are authority figures they are susceptible. We certainly don't want to burden our children with the perceived responsibility for our happiness and well-being.

Although we are supporting our children in developing compassion for others by using self-expression, we need to ensure they do not come to see our needs and emotions as more important than theirs. The needs of both our children and ourselves are equal – we need to strive for win-win solutions.

Until we come naturally from our Buddha heart we often seek solutions outside of ourselves. That is, instead of solving a problem ourselves we seek to modify our children's actions to solve our problems. For example, using the example of the children's noise hindering our TV watching, we could find other solutions without involving them. As long as their behaviour was appropriate, but just a little too loud for us to hear the TV, we could choose to go to another TV set (many homes have more than one); we could choose to use headphones; or we could choose to join in with our children and share some quality time and fun. All of these solutions would allow our children to see that we can find solutions in many different ways.

In this last example of TV watching, what message would we like our children to get – that TV is important and even more important than them, or that an opportunity to have fun with them is more important?

5. We often tack more on to the self-expression. We often have difficulty not saying more – not adding blame, demands etc. We lack belief in the self-expression to meet our needs. This is an indication that we are using the self-expression as a means to change our child's behaviour. When we accept responsibility for meeting our needs and when we are not self-cherishing, we will be able to let a self-expression stand alone.

Suggestions:

- Use self-expression selectively.
- Continue to develop your understanding and practice of Buddhism – this provides the appropriate/beneficial worldview and motivation.
- Use only those components of self-expression that are necessary. Less is better than more, since you can add the other components if needed.
- Focus on the three steps you take before you speak. This is crucial. Look deeply into your mind to objectively determine your emotions and needs.
- Find solutions that do not require you to use self-expression.
- Use self-expression for appropriate behaviour and positive emotions and when your needs have been met as well as for inappropriate behaviour and negative emotions.
- Instead of using a self-expression message when your needs aren't being met, sometimes you can pre-empt the situation by giving your children advance information about your intentions eg

"I will need to use the phone at 9, so if you could schedule your calls around that it will help me." or "We have guests coming for dinner tonight, so I need this table clear sometime before 6 o'clock."

Problem Identification and Solution-Focussed Approach

Like the earth and the great elements
And also vast as the immensity of space,
Let me be the living ground
Of love for innumerable beings.

Old scripture

The idea of a problem is in some ways foreign to Buddhist thought. Any situation we find ourselves in is merely a result of past action or karma. Accepting or understanding this means our mind will label a difficult experience as 'the ripening of karma' instead of 'a problem'. This, then means that the way in which we react to the difficulty has changed and the resultant emotions are different. We can also see difficult situations as opportunities to ensure favourable karmic seeds ripen in the future.

Acceptance is fundamental to Buddhism – it is part of the Buddhist worldview. As Buddhists we accept without condemnation our reactions and emotions. This is what is meant by equanimity. We also accept others with the same quality of equanimity. This means we acknowledge the realities of how another person or child can be open to change.

In spite of this general acceptance, Buddhists believe their world is in a constant flux – it is constantly changing. If we are presented with an uncomfortable situation today, it will probably be different tomorrow or the next day. Everything is constantly changing – nothing is permanent.

Buddhists try to accept situations. We usually try to change situations or to solve 'problems'. We have a tendency to see problems instead of opportunities; faults instead of positives; inappropriate behaviour instead of appropriate behaviour. In fact, some of us tend to focus on the negative in every aspect of life. Buddhism leads us away from this kind of thinking and teaches effective ways for generating positive change.

Living in a Western culture with a Western language it is difficult to avoid the word 'problem'.

What is a problem?

Human problems and conflicts ultimately are about unmet needs. But having unmet needs does not constitute a problem. At what point does a problem become a problem? For example, our child is making a noise and we can't hear the person on the phone. We tell our children that the noise is making it difficult to hear on the phone. Our children reduce their noise and we can hear. Was this a problem? I don't think so. But if the children don't reduce the noise, is it a problem then? I think so. It seems a problem exists, not when we have an unmet need but when we can't easily meet that need.

Most of our problems are seen as problems because we expect the outside environment, or the other person, to change in order to meet our needs. We have little control over the outside environment, and total control over our internal environment i.e. our mind. This is another way of saying that we can develop an internal locus of control. For example, we want acceptance so we try to 'fit in' with our social set. We wear the 'right' clothes, go to the 'right' parties, pretend to be something we are not, so that we feel accepted. But we cannot guarantee other people will accept us, and so we are setting ourselves up for suffering. If we accept ourselves and understand the true nature of reality, we can't suffer because of lack of external acceptance.

Another example: Maybe we work in an environment where we are constantly told what to do. We feel our need for autonomy and independence is not met, so we suffer. We want to change the external environment and make people stop telling us what to do. If we have control over our thoughts and feelings we have true autonomy and independence, and other people telling us what to do would not bother us.

Recall the many Tibetan Buddhists who have been imprisoned and physically abused for decades. Did they moan about their problems of lack of autonomy etc.? No. They accepted the situation and used their control of their mind to maintain independence. It is not just Buddhists who have done this. We often hear stories of political prisoners who were incarcerated for years and who came out of the situation with compassion, understanding and wisdom. These people rely on an internal locus of control to determine what they think and how they feel. This kind of control is what we want for our children. We can have it too.

This doesn't mean we allow our child's inappropriate behaviour to continue. Instead we help them to learn compassion and wisdom. What it does mean is that we are trying to see objectively what is happening instead of reacting to what we perceive as a 'problem'.

Often within our family setting, not only do we see too many situations as 'problems', we also tend to want to solve these problems by changing or stopping our child's actions. In most situations this is not the only, or the best, solution. As mentioned earlier, we can take action ourselves instead of expecting others to take action to meet our needs. For example: our children are working on a 500 piece jigsaw puzzle on the dining room table. They have spent all afternoon working on it and are not quite finished when dinner time comes. Their behaviour is appropriate – we have said they can do jigsaw puzzles on the table. They are having fun and want to finish it after dinner. Our usual response may be to make them clear it away so we can have dinner on the table, but we have other options. We could have dinner outside, we could have a picnic on the floor, or we could have dinner later than usual.

All behaviour, including communicating, aims to reduce current needs to tolerable levels i.e. to prevent or solve problems. Most of our psychological needs can be met from within. When a problem arises it is often a problem only because we have not taken responsibility for meeting our needs from within.

Problems have solutions

Often people think they have problems that cannot be solved, but a problem cannot exist without a solution. The concept of solution must be developed before there can be a concept of problem. Without the idea that problems can be solved, there are no problems only 'facts-of-life' i.e. unfortunate occurrences that cannot be avoided or changed.

We need to understand this difference because in one we adopt a solution-focussed approach and in the other we engage in acceptance. This encompasses the essence of the Prayer of Serenity that calls on God to grant the serenity to accept the things that cannot be changed, the courage to change the things that can be changed, and the wisdom to know the difference.

Problems arise when our needs or perceived needs are not easily met. The problems we have in our parenting role involve our children, and perhaps other people such as their friends, teachers, relatives etc. Some of these problems involve interpersonal conflict i.e. we and/or they are experiencing strong negative emotions. Buddhist teachings tell us the deepest roots of conflict are in the perceptions, values and attitudes of the parties involved in the conflict. This directs us to focus on gaining self-awareness and developing self-knowledge.

As we continue to develop our understanding of Buddhism and bring this awareness into our parenting we are engaging in Buddha Heart Parenting. Wisdom is important in parenting.

We need to be engaged Buddhists – we need to be engaged with our children. We need to work on the inner self or mind at the same time as we are gaining and using the skills of Buddha Heart Parenting. Doing this will reduce conflict and reduce problems. We see reality for what it is, and we can respond with wisdom and compassion instead of reacting with emotion and suffering.

We have to better ourselves if we want our children to better themselves.

If we think we can solve a problem, it is easy

Our belief about our ability to solve problems greatly influences how easily we can solve problems. If we believe we can't solve problems then problems are more difficult to solve. Alternately, if we believe we can solve problems, then problems are easier to solve. We can be biased by a lot of things eg the problem statement, previous methods of reaching solution and general knowledge. These biases are habitual ways of thinking and doing which impact on how we solve, or fail to solve, problems.

The teaching of the Buddha expressed in the *Dhammapada*, clearly says that the mind is the maker of all things. Buddhists are seen as people who can take a detached and objective view of a problem and provide sensible solutions based on wisdom and compassion. They have a positive mindset bias.

> The **Dharmmapada** is a collection of 423 verses in Pali uttered by the Buddha on 305 occasions for the benefit of a wide range of people.

Is there a difference between problem-solving and solution-finding?

When we, or our children, have problems we often think we have to engage in *problem solving*. What is more beneficial is to adopt a *solution-focused* approach and to engage in *solution-finding*. This orientation is based on the idea that reality follows where we place our attention. That is, what our mind focuses on is what is most real to us. This means that the more we focus on our problem the more its apparent reality increases. The problem becomes more solid and more of a problem, making it harder to solve.

We are all familiar with learning to ride a bike, or to drive a car, and seeing a post somewhere in front of us. We don't want to run into the post but we keep focusing on it because it is the one thing we don't want to hit. And guess what? We run into the post! Same principle – what we focus on is what is most real to us and what we get.

What is a solution-focused approach?

A solution-focused approach focuses on the positive, on the solution and on the future as we want it to be. It recognizes that change is occurring all the time, nothing is permanent, and small changes can lead to large changes. A solution-focus appreciates that we all have within us the internal resources to solve any problem that may come our way.

One of the most obvious solutions to most problems simply involves someone doing something differently or seeing something differently. Once an expectation becomes different, a pattern can change – mental patterns and behavioural patterns alike.

Problem owners and solution owners

Although it is fraught with danger, an important first step in a solution-focused approach is determining who owns the problem i.e. problem ownership. There are two risks in determining problem ownership: (1) developing an attitude of 'not-my-problem', and (2) finger-pointing.

There is a risk with establishing problem ownership that we free ourselves of responsibility. When others 'own' the problem those who don't own the problem are given implicit permission to step away and think they have no role in solving

the problem. We commonly hear: 'It's his problem, not mine."
If we are compassionate and see someone has a problem we can
have a role in the solution. Another risk in determining
problem ownership is the tendency to blame the person who
owns the problem. This is counter-productive to solving the
problem. It lies in the same mindset as 'who is to blame?'
Instead of finding fault we need to find solutions.

So how do we get around the baggage that tends to go with
the term 'problem ownership'? We could invent new terms for
the various people involved in problems and solving problems,
such as 'problem identifiers' and 'solution owners', but it can
be confusing to remember what these terms mean. I will
continue to use the traditional term 'problem ownership'
whilst making sure it is defined in such a way that allows others
to be an active part of solution-finding.

Determining problem ownership will identify what skills
from Buddha Heart Parenting will be most effective to use
especially in the first instance. The person who owns the
problem will then be one of the solution owners – depending
on the problem, they might be the only solution owner, but we
might all own the solution. It is important to recognise that
'solution owner' is a much more appropriate concept to use
than 'problem owner', because it focuses on there being a
positive outcome.

Who owns the problem?

The general rule of thumb is: if someone's behaviour is
'bothering' us then it is our problem. If we feel angry, upset,
annoyed, sad, etc we own the problem. If our child feels angry,
upset, annoyed, sad, etc they own the problem. If we both feel
one of these emotions we both own the problem situation.

This can be overly simplistic, because we, as parents, will
often feel something when our child has a problem. We even
feel for them when they don't have a problem. For example,
our child has friends over and they exclude her from their play.
We feel hurt and sorry for our child – we feel her rejection. But

it is not our problem. We could be very wrong about the existence of a problem at all. Our child might not mind being excluded from the game, because she doesn't like the game anyway, or she might not mind because she knows that is what happens to everybody sometimes. In this case we may go into solution-finding mode with our child when there is no problem to solve. We could actually create a problem in this instance, by letting our child know that we thought they *should* be upset about being excluded. This occurs more often than we realise.

To be more clear in determining if we have a problem consider the following:

- Do I have a need that is not being met?
- Could someone get hurt?
- Could someone's possessions be at risk of damage?
- Is my child too young to accept responsibility for this problem?

If the answer is 'yes' to any of these questions, we own the problem. If the answers are 'no' to all the questions then our child may have a problem, especially if they are showing signs of anger, sadness etc.

Here are some examples to make it easier to understand problem ownership:

Our 2 year old son is tearing up a magazine. He is clearly enjoying himself. We own the problem, if we are upset.

Our 10 year old son has missed out on selection for the team and is crying. Our son owns the problem.

Our child and her friends make lunch and leave a mess in the kitchen. We own the problem because we are annoyed about the mess. The children don't mind the mess.

Our 12 month old daughter is crying because she is hungry – this is our problem. (She is too young to take responsibility for the problem.)

We see our 5 year old poking his new baby brother with a toy. We own the problem. (Our new baby is too young to own the problem and his safety is at risk.)

At the dinner table our 6 year old son refuses to eat his dinner. An hour later he complains of being hungry. Our son owns the problem.

Our children are fighting but no one is in danger. This is their problem.

What is the process of solution-finding?

What to do when we have the problem

If we own the problem, we start the solution-finding with looking deeply inside to understand the nature of the problem. Objectively consider:

- What is happening?
- What am I feeling?
- What need is unmet?
- What would I like to happen?

We can then consider different solutions:

- Can I meet this need internally?
- Is my need more important than my child's?
- What actions can I take?
- Is there a solution that I can take without involving my child?
- If I am to involve my child in the solution, which Buddha Heart Parenting skill/s will I use eg self-expression, respectful guidance.
- If I am to use self-expression which components are likely to be needed?

If none of these questions lead to desired results we can then enter the 'effect–management' phase of solution-finding.

This is discussed in the next chapter. Most problems will be solved with one of the other options and these options need to be employed first, unless the situation is dangerous and someone or someone's possessions are at risk of harm. In these instances we need to **ensure safety as the highest priority.**

What to do when our child has the problem

Whenever our child is upset, angry, annoyed etc they own the problem. They may become upset, angry etc when we attempt to solve our problem – at which time we both have a problem. Irrespective of whose problem it is, once our child shows emotion we need to use empathic listening. Unless they feel understood they will not be in a position to engage in solution-finding or to seek to understand us, or our position.

Mastering the dual compassionate communication skills of empathic listening and self-expression offers a powerful method of making deep connections and of finding effective solutions. No matter where we are in the solution-focused process, and whether it is our problem or our child's, if either party becomes 'upset' we need to go back to either self-expression if we have the emotion, or empathic listening if our child has the emotion. The skill of swapping between the two skills is one of the most important compassionate communication skills we can have.

Do we always have to find solutions?

Earlier, I said 'if we choose to act' in relation to when our child feels angry, sad etc. This is because acting every time our child has a problem may not be in their best interest. If they have a problem it may be most beneficial to our child to let them handle it themselves. Our aim is to take the action that respects both ourselves and our child. What action we choose to take depends on:

- The age of our child;
- What kind of problem it is; and

- How long the problem has existed or how many times it happens.

Our aim is to support our children in developing skills to solve their own problems. We want them to believe they are able to solve problems. Research has shown that if people think they can solve problems then they can solve problems. If they don't think they can solve problems they are less likely to be able to. So, we need to think before we jump in and help our child solve their problems.

How do we support solution-finding?

If we decide it is in our child's best interests for us to support them in solution-finding, we start with empathic listening. When we listen empathically we often find what we thought was the problem is not the problem at all. For instance, our son comes home from school and says "Boy, I hate school". We reply "Sounds like you had a bad day at school?" "No, school's ok. But on the way to school I tripped on Mr Hercle's hose and broke his sprinkler system. Boy was he mad! Now I have to pay for it."

So our first assumption that he had a bad day at school did not identify the problem. When we use empathic listening we have to be prepared to use it several times until the real problem surfaces. This is a process similar to peeling an onion. Be prepared for emotions, sometimes strong emotions, and even for the subject to shift to different layers.

Sometimes we may never know what the problem was, because the very act of seeking to understand and listening empathically is enough for our child to be able to go beyond their emotions and see the problem objectively. When this happens they either see there was no real problem or they see the solution easily. In these situations, if the child seems happy after we have listened we don't have to know the details.

At other times they will need help in solution-finding.

When emotional arousal is too high there is no thinking. Strong emotion locks us into a one-dimensional trance. It can be a positive or a negative emotion. For example, when we are in love we have a strong emotion and we can't think clearly about the person – we see them with rose coloured glasses. As the emotional arousal level drops then we can see the person more clearly with all their faults.

We have to help our child to drop their emotional level before we can help them.

What is 'reflective reframing'?

We help our child lower their emotional level by empathic listening combined with reflective reframing. **Reflective reframing** involves putting a different frame or perception on events so the problem is seen as temporary or solvable. We combine empathic listening with reframing so that statements are:

- temporary (so far, yet, up till now);
- in the past;
- emotionally dilute;
- an impression rather than a fact.

For example: "I hate Jim" becomes "Jim is not your favourite person just now". And "I'll never understand this" becomes "This isn't clear to you yet".

When we are having a hard time we often see the world or things as being:

Permanent – we forget that all things are impermanent and that there is constant change. A problem today can be gone tomorrow.

Personal – we tend to take things personally as if the other person or our child is trying to attack us personally. Their behaviour is a result of their met or unmet needs.

Pervasive – a problem can seem to take on great importance and seems to colour other aspects of our life as well.

Reflective reframing helps to dispel these false perceptions. Reflective reframing works outside the conscious mind and is crucial to helping our child move forward. We need to support them to expand their perception and open them to move into the future.

Helping children to imagine the future

When we feel our child has clearly enunciated the problem and is free of emotion we can move into the next phase in the solution-focused approach, i.e. help our child to be clear about how they want things to be different. Help them to describe what they want instead of the problem.

A problem cannot be solved with the same kind of thinking that created the problem. If children don't move from problem-focus to solution-focus and if they continue to examine the problem in greater depth, it will only 'make the hole deeper'.

It can be useful to get our child to think about what two videos would look like: one that was made now and one that was made in a week or a month when the problem no longer exists. What would be the difference between the two? What would be in the one in the future? What would they see there that would show that things had changed? If our child can describe a preferred future, they can achieve it.

What we are doing is nudging our child like a snowball to the top of the hill, from where they can propel themselves downhill, gaining speed and snow as they go.

Helping children decide how to get their vision of the future

Next, we can ask our child what kinds of things they can do now to move things towards their preferred future. Collect as many ideas as possible. As much as possible we can allow our child to make suggestions. We need to resist the temptation to give suggestions unless the child has run out of ideas and we feel there are some good ones she has missed, or unless our child is young and inexperienced in this sort of problem. If, as a last resort, we add a suggestion, we can do it in a way that allows the child to accept or reject it. Perhaps say:

"What do you think would happen if you ...?"
or
"Have you thought about ...?"

When we feel there are sufficient possible suggested actions that would achieve their preferred future, we ask them which one or ones they think would be most appropriate. For example, we could say:

"Which of these ideas do you think would give the results you want?"

When they have chosen one, or some, possible actions, ask them:

"What do you think would happen if you did ...?"

This is a crucial step in the solution-focused approach. Unless they think through what would happen they may end up with a bigger problem or else discouraged because nothing has changed. Talk them through their suggestions until they appear to have settled on what they want to do.

When they have decided what actions they want to take, get them to mentally rehearse (sometimes they could physically rehearse – role play) these actions to feel confident and to pattern the new actions. We can help them to set a plan for when they will take the actions and a time for review of their plan. This is an important part of the solution-focused approach to make sure they know they will have support if they need it.

If we see any change in the situation for the better we could use feedback to help our child know they are starting to get results. Small changes in the right direction can be amplified to great effect.

No problem is so great that you can't ignore it or walk away from it.

Encouraging Self-Discipline

The thought manifests as the word;
The word manifests as the deed;
The deed develops into habit;
And habit hardens into character;
So watch the thought and its ways with care,
And let it spring from love
Born out of concern for all beings....

As the Shadow follows the body,
As we think, so we become.

Dhammapada

This section provides us with skills and knowledge on how to help our children to develop self-discipline. It also provides us with skills to guide our child to behave appropriately.

- **Supporting Self-Discipline and Using Respectful Guidance**

- **Effect-Management**

Supporting Self-Discipline and Using Respectful Guidance

Better than a meaningless story of a thousand words
Is a single word of deep meaning
Which, when heard, produces peace.

Dhammapada

Buddha Heart Parenting focuses on wisdom and compassion, and on the use of wisdom and compassion to support our children to develop and express their Buddha nature. Buddha Heart Parenting provides us with skills to enable this process, especially through supporting self-discipline and using Respectful Guidance.

What is discipline?

Most parenting styles emphasise discipline and teach methods of disciplining children. They rely on discipline to instil appropriate behaviours and attitudes in children. Although 'discipline' comes from a Latin word meaning to 'educate' especially in matters of conduct, its use in terms of child behaviour mostly refers to punishment and consequences. Buddha Heart Parenting sees discipline as a positive means by which children learn compassion and appropriate behaviours and gain the skill of making wise decisions when confronted with problems. That is, it supports them in developing self-discipline.

Regardless of which parenting style parents use (apart from Buddha Heart Parenting), when they discipline their child most parents use discipline that provides a negative outcome for inappropriate behaviour. Children do not need negative outcomes to learn what is inappropriate behaviour, nor to learn how to engage in appropriate behaviour. Negative outcomes are unpleasant. We don't feel good when we have a negative outcome – neither do our children. Research and life experiences show us that we learn better and quicker when we have pleasant experiences. Why then, do we insist that we must discipline our children with negative outcomes in this way? Negative outcomes need to be a final stage if all other strategies fail.

Are natural and logical consequences appropriate?

There was a strong movement away from reward and punishment in the 1970s with teachers, trainers and counsellors encouraging parents to turn to natural and logical consequences. A natural consequence is one that occurs without our intervention. For example, our child goes outside in cold weather in a singlet and shorts – the natural consequence is she will get cold. We can let natural consequences happen as long as no one's safety is at risk. Natural consequences allow children to experience cause and effect – the natural and universal law.

Logical consequences, on the other hand, are consequences that a parent or caregiver designs. These consequences may be positive consequences eg when our child finishes their homework they can play outside. Or they can be negative eg our child plays with a ball in the house and we remove the ball for a week. The consequence needs to be logically related to the behaviour eg if our child stays out later than the agreed time, they are grounded for a period of time. Or if they ride their bike on the road their bike is put away for a few days. Without a logical connection to the inappropriate behaviour, consequences become arbitrary and are viewed by our child as punishment. For example, if our child rides their bike on the road we tell them they will miss TV for the rest of the week.

At face value, there is nothing wrong with logical consequences. They are a valuable way to help our child understand dependent origination and other fundamental principles of Buddhism. The problem is that very few parents can use them in a detached manner that allows their child to see that the consequence is just the playing out of the cause–effect relationship, even if the effect is contrived. In all my years as a parenting educator and counsellor, I have seen few parents who have the worldview or mindset to use this skill as it was intended, without a lot of inner work taking place first.

Parents use logical consequences as a form of punishment – and therefore, in the child's mind, it is no different from punishment. Regardless of how perfectly these parents word the logical consequence choice, their intention and motivation is to make the child do what they say, and for the child to know that if they don't do as they say there will be an unpleasant consequence following. For example, the choice is:

"You can stay inside and play quietly or if you want to continue to kick the ball you can do it outside",

And then the consequence is:

"Since you are still playing with the ball in the house, you cannot have your ball, and you cannot go outside to play for a week."

There is nothing particularly wrong with the words. But when parents give these choices and consequences as a means to control their children, their children will view this approach as an attempt at power and control and will react accordingly.

Some parents over-use logical consequences. They have the mistaken belief that they have to discipline their children and so logical consequences are used for everything. They become a means to control their children. The consequences may still be logical but they are used when other Buddha Heart Parenting skills would be more appropriate.

In some ways logical consequences are more destructive than punishment because they are used under the guise of cooperation and fairness, but they become covert manipulation. At least punishment is promoted as punishment. There are no mixed messages.

How do we encourage self-discipline?

Buddha Heart Parenting assumes parents are engaged Buddhists. That is, it assumes parents are striving to deepen their understanding and practice of Buddhist principles and concepts, whilst at the same time striving to incorporate compassion and wisdom into skills and strategies, which support their children to connect and develop their Buddha nature/heart. Buddha Heart Parenting skills and strategies provide a model for our children of how to integrate compassion and wisdom into daily life.

When we use Buddha Heart Parenting, we have a range of options to encourage appropriate behaviour and to deal with inappropriate behaviour. We can use:

Feedback. Feedback provides verifiable feedback to our children to support them to develop an internal locus of control. Feedback also helps our child develop the skill of self-encouragement. Using this skill focuses on the positive and on the potential that our child has. If we can help our child develop an internal frame of reference or locus of control, they will behave appropriately simply because that is what feels best to do.

Empathic listening. Empathic listening allows our child to look deeply within herself to understand her needs and feelings/emotions as a first step towards meeting those needs. It helps her to be resourceful. Empathic listening allows our child to see the world and their experiences objectively.

Self-expression. Self-expression provides us with a respectful compassionate method to express our needs and feelings/emotions to our child. We model for our child how to do this, so they, in turn, can use self-expression to express their needs and feelings/emotions.

Solution-Focus. When we use a solution-focused approach to problem solving we help our children to see their hidden resources and give them an approach that acknowledges that there is constant change and nothing is permanent.

Respectful Guidance. Respectful Guidance is a tool which we can use to support our child to know what are appropriate behaviours and how and why to engage in them.

Effect-management. Effect-management is a tool to support our child to deepen her understanding of cause and effect, to develop compassion for others, and to develop skills in making choices based on wisdom.

All these skills and strategies complement our continuing study of Buddhism and support us in 'walking the talk' or being 'engaged Buddhists'. The skills and strategies without the underlying Buddhist intention and motivation may be no different to other techniques, and may end up as just a means to control our children. So it is important that we use this two-pronged approach.

The two skills and strategies listed above that we haven't discussed in detail are Respectful Guidance and Effect-Management. Respectful Guidance is explained here and Effect-Management is dealt with in the next chapter.

What is Respectful Guidance?

Respectful Guidance is a tool we can use to help our child learn appropriate behaviour. This tool allows children to develop their inner guidance system so they can function responsibly by themselves. Respectful Guidance aims to guide a child's behaviour on a daily basis whilst at the same time supporting them to become self-disciplined and compassionate.

Often inappropriate behaviour is our child's way of telling us they need help in directing their behaviour, and it provides us with an opportunity to teach new behaviour. If we see inappropriate behaviour in this light we are in a positive headspace with positive emotion and with an intention to guide our child. When we have this intention and motivation our underlying attitude is one of respect and so we can easily give our child Respectful Guidance.

Respectful Guidance is simple. Once we have the attitude, the words come easily. If we have some strong patterning that uses control, blaming, nagging, 'helping', threatening, sarcasm, etc we may need to study the examples in this chapter and take them into our meditation and rehearse them. Practice makes perfect. We may need time to develop new patterns, but if they are supported by an underlying attitude change it will happen in no time at all.

How do we use Respectful Guidance?

Respectful Guidance is not just one single thing we do or say, it encompasses a range of things we can do and/or say to respectfully guide our child to adopt appropriate behaviour. What we do depends on the circumstances, the age of our child etc.

We have the following skills and strategies to choose from:

Develop clear guidelines
Explain appropriate behaviour
Provide feedback for appropriate behaviour
Ignore inappropriate behaviour

Avoid 'no' and 'don't'
Review and redirect
Seek solutions
Prevent
Distract
Provide opportunities to develop sound decision making skills

Develop clear guidelines.

No matter what the age of our child we need to have a minimum number of clear guidelines. These guidelines need to be reasonable and in line with our child's age. If we have too many guidelines our children are liable to forget them, and they may also feel too restricted. We may also forget them if we have too many. It is important to remember that our home is our children's home too and it needs to be a suitable environment for them. If they can't play, explore, have friends over, etc because of the fragility of our furnishings or lack of space etc it is **our** home not theirs.

Depending on the age of our child, it is beneficial to set the guidelines with them. After all, the guidelines apply to everyone living in the house, and our child may have some suggestions about behaviour and situations that affect them. If they are part of the decision making, they are more likely to stick to the guidelines.

We can make sure the guidelines are simple and clear. We need to follow through consistently to ensure the guidelines are held.

An important point we often forget is, the guidelines apply to everyone, not just our child. If the guideline is 'food is to be eaten in the kitchen and dining room only', then we cannot sit down in the lounge room in front of the TV and eat a snack. Double standards are neither respectful nor fair, and our children will pick up on this very quickly.

Clearly explain appropriate behaviour.

Many times we tell our child what **not to do**, not what **to do**. We may think it is obvious what is appropriate behaviour, but from a child's perspective it isn't. When we tell our children what not to do we are reinforcing the negative, inappropriate behaviour with negative comments. These don't feel good. Remember, when a child feels better they do better.

Some examples of negative comments and how they can be changed to positive instructions:

Negative.....	Positive.....
Don't drop your rubbish.	*Put your rubbish in the bin.*
Stop hitting the dog.	*Pat the dog gently.*
Stop fighting.	*You could take turns.*
Don't play with your food.	*Eat your dinner.*
Stop squirting water.	*Squirt the water outside.*
Don't leave your clothes there.	*Put your clothes in your room.*

Our intention is that our child will understand what is expected of him in different social situations. Our supportive tone of voice will convey this intention. Positive statements promote a positive environment for learning and nurturing self-esteem.

Provide feedback for appropriate behaviour.

Remember how powerful feedback can be to develop self-encouragement in children, and to instil appropriate behaviour? This is an important way we can respectfully guide our children's behaviour. We need to be careful not to overuse feedback, but its judicious use helps our children immensely.

For example:

> *"You've put your toys away. That will make vacuuming easier."*
> *"You remembered to feed the dog."*

"You shared your chips with your sister."
"See how happy he was when you helped him."

Ignore inappropriate behaviour

An important skill we can use to respectfully guide our child's behaviour is to ignore inappropriate behaviour. Many parents have difficulty doing this as they feel that to ignore inappropriate behaviour is to agree with it. This is not the case. Many inappropriate behaviours are done to get our attention or simply to 'try them on' to see what will happen. As long as nobody's safety is threatened, many are best ignored. When ignored they will usually cease.

When we make a decision to ignore an inappropriate behaviour our child has been using for sometime we need to let our child know that in future we will ignore this behaviour. The best time to tell them is when they are doing something else – not the inappropriate behaviour. We may give them a reason why we will be ignoring their behaviour, and make it clear that it is the behaviour we are ignoring and not them. For example we may something like:

"Many times when I tell you that you can't do something, you will talk in a whining voice asking me over and over to let you do it. In the past I have been telling you over and over again that you can't do the thing. I now realise that this is not beneficial to either of us, and I realise I haven't been treating you respectfully at these times. I would like our relationship to be better. In future when you talk in a whining voice in these situations I will ignore your behaviour."

Consistency is important. This may be difficult at first and we may only remember after we have started our usual response. On these occasions we can say to our child:

"I made a mistake and forgot to ignore your behaviour."
And then ignore it.

New behaviours that extinguish quickly when ignored are:

Swearing
Spitting
Tantrums
Whining
Complaining
Genital play and masturbation in young children
Siblings fighting (unless safety (physical, emotional or mental) is threatened)

Sibling fighting and bickering is very common and causes concern to many parents. Most fights between siblings are merely annoying squabbles and when we intervene it just delays the process of the children working it out for themselves.

Fighting is often an effective but destructive way for children to gain our attention, and remember, for some children negative attention is better than none at all. When children fight or argue we have a tendency to want to know who started it – as if that can be determined? When we launch in and inadvertently take sides we are setting up victims and bullies.

If we are going to ignore our children fighting we need to provide them with the skills to solve their problems amicably. We can do this by modelling problem solving each time we have a problem with another person's behaviour or with their behaviour. If we bicker and fight with others eg our partner or mother, our child learns that this is what you do when there is a difference of opinion.

At a time when our children aren't fighting, we can talk to them about ways they could avoid fighting and increase joint cooperation. Using a solution focus to get them to come up with solutions and desired outcomes will provide them with a process, too.

Occasionally parents choose to ignore their children's fighting as the easy way out. Sometimes these parents have learnt that sibling fighting is the children's problem and so they ignore it. At first glance, this is appropriate action for the parent to take. But in some situations when we look closer we see that the children are missing an opportunity to learn cooperation and respect. Here is an example:

> *Jacinta did a parenting course and learnt that if parents ignore their children's squabbling and fighting the children will learn to work things out for themselves. She decided to do this. But she failed to look at the situation clearly and failed to look at the children's needs. There had been a history of fighting, or abuse, from the time the second baby was born and came home from hospital. Her daughter would treat her new brother like a toy – always wanting to pick him up and carry him around. Jacinta thought this was 'lovely' and she thought her daughter really loved her brother.*
>
> *In time it became clear that the new brother was a toy as he was poked and pulled along by an arm or leg. Over the following months the younger brother learnt that he had to laugh when this happened because crying didn't bring mum to his rescue, and only made his sister abuse him more.*
>
> *By the time the younger child was two years old the children would fight constantly, with the bigger one becoming violent. Still mum did nothing.*

What Jacinta failed to realise was that she wasn't teaching her children to sort it out for themselves. She was teaching them that if you are bigger you can impose your will on someone else, and teaching them that violence is OK. The younger brother was learning that mum was not going to be there to protect him when he needed it.

Although it is appropriate to ignore sibling squabbling and fighting this must be accompanied with Respectful Guidance that teaches children ways to cooperate and find compassionate and respectful ways to solve their differences. At all times bigger children must be stopped from physically abusing younger children. If we don't stop a bully being a bully they will always be a bully. If we don't stop bullying and help the 'victim' find ways of compassionately dealing with the situation, they may always be 'victims'. Through ignorance this mother was not acting with compassion or wisdom.

Avoid 'no' and 'don't'.

We all get tired of being told 'no' and 'don't'. When these words are overused our child may not react to a 'no' or 'don't' in a situation where they are in danger. They will have become desensitised to the words. Anything we say to our child that includes these words can be turned to a positive. We can think of what we want our child to do, not what we don't want them to do.

Review and Redirection

Review and redirection provide Respectful Guidance to our children as they learn appropriate behaviour. Review and redirection is a compassionate communication skill that provides the following outcomes:

- **acknowledges** the child's need or what they are wanting to do,
- **describes** what else is happening in the environment that may preclude them from meeting their need, and
- **provides** a solution or an alternative, in either time or activity.

  The first two outcomes provide a *review* for our child of

- what they want; and
- what others want, or what is happening that may prevent them getting what they want;

The last outcome provides *redirection*. In light of what else is happening in the environment, either the activity our child wants to do is moved to a future time, or an alternative activity is suggested.

Putting the three parts of review and redirection together looks like this:

1. **Acknowledge** that we recognise what our child wants to do. For example,

   "You want to be picked up ..... ."
   "You want to play with the ball ..... ."
   "You want to play with Jake ...."

2. **Describe** what else is happening in the environment. For example,

   "You want to be picked up. I need to finish cutting the vegies for dinner."
   "You want to play with the ball. There are a lot of fragile things in here."
   "You want to play with Jake. He is studying for a test."

3. **Provide** a solution or an alternative. For example,

   "You want to be picked up. I need to finish cutting the vegies for dinner. I can pick you up in a minute."
   "You want to play with the ball. There are a lot of fragile things in here. You could play with it outside."
   "You want to play with Jake. He is studying for a test. I would love to play with you."

In some situations review and redirection might take the following form:

"Peta wants to keep playing with that toy. Here's one for you."
"Blocks are not for throwing. Let's build a tower with them."
"The cat doesn't like to be hit. Pat her gently, like this."
"The ice-cream will melt on the bench. Put it in the freezer."

Seek Solutions

In some situations where our child has an inappropriate behaviour that they have displayed for some time, perhaps months or years, it may be beneficial to do a solution seeking activity with them. If we have other children we could bring them in on this activity too. This way everyone in the family can own the solution to some degree, and our child can feel that everyone is trying to help them. This support and positive expectation provides a valuable motivation for change.

We can get everyone involved in brainstorming solutions. Children are amazingly resourceful and will come up with creative and useful ways to develop appropriate behaviour. For example, one of my children repeatedly forgot to take her shoes off before she entered the house. She and her brothers came up with the following possible solutions:

- Put a sign on the outside of the door to tell people to take off their shoes;
- Lock the doors so people are reminded to take their shoes off before they enter;
- Everyone else puts their shoes in front of the door so the child will have to walk over them to get to the door – this will trigger their memory;
- Buy a frog sensor and program it to say: "Please take off your shoes"
- Buy a frog sensor that croaks when someone comes to the door – this will remind everyone to take off their shoes;
- Paint footprints that lead to the shoe rack beside the door;

As we can see all these suggested solutions focus on 'helping' our child do better in the future. This is much different to focussing on the inappropriate behaviour and developing a linked or negotiated-effect.

Once the brainstormed list is developed, our child could then pick the solution that they think would work for them. We need to make sure there are no safety issues.

In the situation with my child, she chose the solution: "Everyone else puts their shoes in front of the door so she had to walk over them to get to the door". It looked a bit messy on our front landing with all the shoes in front of the door, but it worked, and we only had to have the shoes there for a few weeks.

Prevention is the best course of action

Most times it is more advisable to prevent inappropriate behaviour from occurring than to attempt to deal with it later. We can do this by arranging the physical environment so that both we and our children can meet our needs easily. Children need sufficient resources to engage their mind and body. Spending quality time with our children gives them the confidence to know that they are valued.

Use distraction

Small children have difficulty taking their focus off a situation. If they want something, they want it **now**, even if we explain that it is someone else's toy/possession or that it is dangerous. In these situations we can respectfully guide our child's behaviour by distracting them with other things or activities until their desire has decreased. This way the situation does not escalate to the stage where it is difficult for them to learn appropriate behaviour.

It often works to distract a child with a similar outcome. For example, if they wanted to play with another child's toy, they may be distracted with a similar toy. The desired object may need to be removed from the child's view, as young children are often unable to understand why they can't have what they see.

Provide a model.

One of the most crucial methods of helping our child develop appropriate behaviour is to provide them with a good model. Despite what we say, and despite how we correct them, our children are likely to adopt our behaviours. They subconsciously or even consciously look for congruency between what we expect of them and what we do ourselves.

Provide opportunities to develop sound decision making skills.

In developing appropriate behaviour, children have to make choices. They have to choose how to act or behave in any situation. When our child is around her peers she is given an example of how she could behave. She is also given clear messages of how she could behave from TV and videos. How does our child choose what is appropriate? Children who do not have opportunities to make choices from an early age find it difficult when confronted with compelling arguments from their peers or from the media.

We can support our children to make wise decisions by giving them lots of experience in making choices from the time they are very young. We can ask a young child questions like:

"How many books would you like me to read you tonight, one or two?"
"Do you want to walk or be carried?"
"Would you like to wear these shorts or these long pants?"

The more practice children have in weighting up the pros and cons of each possible choice the more easily they will be able to do it when they are older. And the more easily they will make decisions based on compassion and wisdom too.

More information on how to build decision making skills in our child is provided in a later chapter.

The skills and strategies outlined so far will work to support our child to develop self-discipline and appropriate behaviour. They also work to build and enhance connected relationships and joyous families. We will use these skills and strategies in our everyday life with our child. In the next chapter we look at effect-management. Effect-management is a strategy we use when other skills and strategies don't result in the necessary change in behaviour.

Effect-Management

Those who see worldly life as an obstacle to Dharma
See no Dharma in everyday actions;
They have not yet discovered
That there are no everyday actions outside of Dharma.
Thirteenth Century Zen Master Dogen

There are times when compassionate communication, Respectful Guidance and other strategies outlined in earlier chapters do not result in cessation of inappropriate behaviour. At these times we need to support our children to deepen their understanding of cause and effect, to develop compassion for others, and to develop skills in making choices based on wisdom.

What is effect-management?

Effect-management is based on one of the core concepts in Buddhism ie dependent origination or the principle of cause and effect. Dependent origination highlights the concept of inter-dependency of existence. Buddha described dependent origination as a natural law, a fundamental truth that exists independently of our existence – whether we exist or not this law applies.

It is very simple and easy to understand. One reaps what one sows. You get what you give. Every effect has its cause.

We also know that there is more than one factor involved in determining a result. We call these other factors 'conditions'. Cause and condition can be likened to the process of germination. The seed (cause) needs water, fertiliser and sunlight (conditions) in order to germinate.

The part condition plays can be understood when we consider: a skilful deed done now can be the cause of a beneficial effect in the future, or it can be a condition for preventing a bad effect of a bad cause in the past. Even if this bad effect does come it will generally be less severe, because of the beneficial deed in the present. Moreover since cause cannot come in effect without condition(s), it is important to understand that although we cannot change the cause and effect, we can change the conditions. This is why Buddhism emphasises that if we want to change our fate we need to change the condition.

This is all a bit abstract without an example to illustrate how it works. Suppose in the past (either in this lifetime or previous ones) we have acted unskilfully many times by stealing. We would therefore expect many bad effects now or in the future. These bad effects might be that no-one trusts us or we are not given responsibility for managing money, or money is stolen from us. But if we now live our life with compassion and wisdom and are generous with our money and treat other people's money and possessions with respect, then these bad effects are less likely to come into being. This is because the conditions for them to appear are not present – or are present to a lesser extent.

Dependent origination looks simple. But in fact, it is very deep and profound, especially when it is applied to our daily life. Understanding dependent origination provides the foundation for effect-management strategies in Buddha Heart Parenting. Effect-management supports our child to understand dependent origination and provides her with the means to live within the law to actualise their Buddha nature/heart. Without this understanding and motivation we may use effect-management to punish or control our child – this is not the intention and it is counterproductive to do so.

Effect-management helps our child learn cause-effect and responsible compassionate action. We act in a compassionate way to help them understand the effects of their behaviour.

There are different kinds of effects

Within effect-management strategies there are three types of effects our child can experience as a result of their behaviour:

The first type is simple **cause-effect**. This is similar to the actions of karma. Karma refers to imprints on the mind and the effects of these imprints. It functions in a similar way as material cause and effect. Cause-effect is sometimes called natural consequences. It occurs when we do nothing and our child experiences the effects of their behaviour. Examples are:

Our child leaves her book in the garden when it is going to rain. The effect is the book is ruined. **or**
Our child refuses to take lunch to school and he experiences hunger. **or**
Our child is rude to her friend and she loses the friendship.

Most times simple cause-effect is the best way for children to learn. It is often difficult for us, as parents, to allow simple cause-effect to happen because we don't want our child to suffer. But sometimes, temporary suffering provides the learning so that more suffering is prevented in the future.

We should never allow cause-effect to happen when there is any risk to our child or any other person. Safety is always the first priority.

The second type of effect is **negotiated-effect**. We use negotiated-effects when the following criteria are met:

- when our child has a history of an inappropriate behaviour,
- simple cause-effect is not appropriate, and
- self-expression, respectful guidance, and other skills of Buddha Heart Parenting have not helped them to change.

In negotiated-effects we negotiate with our child to find an agreed effect that they will experience if they use a certain inappropriate behaviour again. In order to help our child learn about the principle of Cause and Effect it is best if the effect is linked with the behaviour in some way. For example, every day when our child comes home from school she changes into her good clothes and goes out to play. The clothes get dirty and sometimes torn or stained. Together we might decide that if the good clothes are worn out to play and get torn or stained, our child will contribute to the cost of new clothes out of her pocket money.

The third type of effect is a **linked-effect**. A linked-effect is an effect that we create when our child behaves inappropriately. We may use this kind of effect when our child's behaviour is threatening either their safety or someone else's or when there is not sufficient time to agree to a negotiated effect. Linked-effects are not negotiated. They are unilateral, and top-down. For example, our son is kicking a ball in our friend's house when we are visiting. We use self expression but he continues to do it. Our friends have no children and their house contains many breakables. We take the ball and tell our son he cannot have it for a few days because he is not being careful of other people's possessions.

The difference between a linked-effect and punishment lies in our motivation. Is our motivation to help our child or is it to control our child?

Use other skills and strategies first

As we mentioned before, linked- or negotiated-effects need to be one of the last tools in our Buddha Heart Parenting toolkit that we use, or that we use only after careful consideration. We have to be sure that they are the most appropriate option and that we are operating from our Buddha heart. It is very easy to fall into the trap of using effect-management to make our children do what we want. Old ways of thinking and the culture around us strongly focus on using negative deterrents rather than positive respectful guidance to create changes in our children.

Focus on supporting change

When we are coming from a punitive perspective we are aiming to make our child pay for past behaviour. If they have behaved inappropriately, it is now in the past, even if it happened just a minute ago, it is still in the past. When we come from our Buddha heart we are looking at the future and have a solution focus that is aimed at helping our child to find ways to behave appropriately in the future.

All the tools and skills in Buddha Heart Parenting that we have talked about so far, build strong connections with our child and encourage compassion and cooperation. They are the ones to be used routinely, leaving effect-management for occasional use.

Of the three effect-management options simple cause-effect is the most effective one, as it follows the natural law of cause and effect as outlined in Buddhist philosophy. The other two are contrived, artificial and require us as implementers to make sure our child experiences them. This puts us in a delicate position where we have to maintain a balance between wisdom and compassion. We need to ensure we are coming from our Buddha heart. This can be done but we need to check where we are coming from, not just at the outset of dealing with the behaviour, but during the process as well. It is very easy to use effect-management to try to make our child change their behaviour.

More on negotiated-effect...

When parents ask their children what they think would be a suitable effect for their inappropriate behaviour, they are often surprised at the severity of the suggested effects. Even when parents open the discussion by explaining that effects are designed to help people learn appropriate behaviour, and that the effect has to have a connection to the inappropriate behaviour, children still suggest harsh effects, such as; no food for a week or sleeping outside for a month.

Even in the most democratic, respectful families children have not escaped the cultural conditioning that dictates we punish inappropriate behaviour. They are exposed to this way of thinking in schools, at friends' homes, and in the media. It is not surprising that they need guidance in coming up with suitable effects. Rather than dismiss our child's suggestions of possible effects we can steer the suggestions towards less punitive effects, and more supportive ones.

Remember if we collectively decide on an effect for a certain inappropriate behaviour, then we are subject to that effect too. For example, if there is a negotiated-effect for swearing then if we swear we too have to experience the effect.

More on linked-effect...

We use linked-effects in situations where all other ways of encouraging appropriate behaviour have failed or in situations where either it is not appropriate to negotiate or there is not the time to do it. If we have used all other Buddha Heart Parenting strategies and they have failed to encourage appropriate behaviour then the use of a linked-effect is not likely to work very well either. But sometimes action needs to be taken.

Parenting through our Buddha heart builds relationships and builds deep connections with our children. When relationships are sound and there is a deep connection, chronic or long-term inappropriate behaviour will disappear or lessen considerably with the use of the strategies. This does not mean that our children will be angels all the time – they won't. What it does mean is that our children will be cooperative and compassionate and any inappropriate behaviour will usually be short lived and will respond to compassionate communication and respectful guidance.

Children will have bad days, when the external environment impinges on them and they may choose to act-out at home. Remember a happy, fulfilled child behaves appropriately – an unhappy, child who doesn't feel good about themselves will behave inappropriately. When we punish or treat our child harshly because of their inappropriate behaviour they will feel worse and therefore their inappropriate behaviour may increase.

Linked-effects start with choices that we give our child. A choice helps our child to see that they are in control of what happens. Using the ball-throwing example, which appears in several places in the book, it might go like this:

Our home has a guideline that balls are not to be thrown inside the house, and yet our children are throwing a ball in the lounge. We could give them a choice as follows:

"You can stay inside and play a different game or if you want to play with the ball you can do it outside."

Depending on the ages of the children we could leave it at that or if they are young we could add:

"You can decide which you want to do."

At this point we leave the room for a minute or two. By leaving, we give the children time to make the decision for themselves, without feeling like we are going to make them do something.

Most likely they will either find another game that is suitable for indoors or they will go outside to play with the ball. If they continue to play with the ball in the lounge, we could intercept the ball and say:

"Looks like you have decided to play outside, I'll put the ball outside ready for you."

If our relationship with our children is good they will take this as reasonable action and go outside or play a suitable game inside. If they get the ball and bring it back inside to play it is an indication that they may feel a power imbalance in the relationship with you and wish to exert some control. If this is the case, we could back out of the situation at that time, and work to build the relationship.

If we wanted to, we could wait until they have finished playing and have left the room and then remove the ball. We then tell them that we have put the ball away because it was being used irresponsibly and they can have the ball again in three days, at which time they have the opportunity to use it responsibly. If the ball is out of sight they will usually accept this decision.

Because there is a fine line between implementing linked-effects and punishment, we need to be very clear we are operating out of our Buddha heart. This cannot be stressed enough.

Deciding on linked-effects for different inappropriate behaviours in different situations becomes easier with practice. Below are a few examples of possible linked-effects for a problem faced by many parents.

Our child is not eating the evening meal that we prepared. This is a good time to let cause-effect happen ie our child will be hungry later. But our child comes into the kitchen later and gets biscuits out of the cupboard and eats them. If this is a once-off event it needs either ignoring or self-expression or a solution focused approach, but if it has become routine we could:

> **Discuss the dinner menu** with our child to make sure that within the week's meals there are sufficient that she likes and are of her choosing.
>
> **Explain our concern** that she eats a balanced nutritious diet.
>
> Agree on a **negotiated-effect** if she doesn't eat her meal.
>
> Then, when our child refuses to eat dinner we could **give her the choice** of eating the food that has been prepared or of experiencing the negotiated, agreed effect.
>
> In the meantime we have removed all snack food from the kitchen, so that should she attempt to eat snack food later, she will find nothing.

> *Every behaviour has a positive intention.*
> *All behaviour is an attempt to meet a need.*

Supporting Self-Realisation for Your Child and for Yourself

You are the Buddha. You are the truth. Then why do you not feel it? Why don't you know it through and through? Because there is a veil in the way, which is attachment to appearances, such as the belief that you are not Buddha, that you are a separate individual, an ego. If you cannot remove this veil all at once, then it must be dissolved gradually.

If you have seen through it totally, even one glimpse, then you can see through it at any time. Wherever you are, whatever presents itself, however things seem to be; simply refer to that ever-present, spacious openness and clarity.

Kalu Rinpoche

This final section presents more skills and strategies that create self-empowered, resilient children and capable decision makers It shows us how to develop connected relationships with our children. The final chapter in this section helps to set realistic goals for ourselves and reminds us to have compassion for ourselves as well as for others.

• **How to Create Self-Empowered Children and Capable Decision Makers**

• **Building Resilient Children and Connected Relationships With Your Children**

• **Have Compassion for Yourself**

How to Create
Self-Empowered Children and
Capable Decision Makers

How wonderful!
How wonderful!
All things are
Perfect
Exactly as they are!

Buddha

One of our aims in parenting is to support our children to be self-empowered. We can't empower them – only they can empower themselves. What we can do is give them the opportunity to become empowered, and provide them with the skills and tools to do it. To be empowered, children need skills in compassionate communication, solution finding, and decision making, and they need life skills in general. They also need to have strong self-esteem, and an understanding that they are in charge of their life, and that their actions result in effects. They need to have an understanding of Buddhist philosophy and have developed compassion and wisdom, which they can apply in daily living. They can have this understanding even if they have never read the Dharma or meditated or been to a temple or even if they are not familiar with the Buddhist terminology.

In this book we have looked in detail at the skills of compassionate communication, solution finding, respectful guidance, effect-management and we have looked at how to support our child in understanding the foundational concepts in Buddhism such as dependent origination. When we use the skills outlined in this book our child will learn these skills for themselves and the skills will help them learn compassion and wisdom. The skill we have not discussed directly so far, is decision making, although the solution finding process is a decision making process in itself.

Decision making is an important skill

One of the most important skills we can teach our children is the skill of wise decision making.

The right to participate in decisions that affect our life is a fundamental human right. In recent years children's rights in wider society have increased and there is now a strong presumption that they 'should' be involved in decisions on matters that directly affect them such as in areas of law and public policy, and within professional practice in case conferences etc. Without the skills and experience in decision making they are often not equipped to do this.

How do we build decision making skills in our child?

Decision making is a skill that can, and is, developed with opportunity, guidance and practice. It is an important skill to learn because we make decisions every day – some big, some small. There are several ways we can support our child to make wise decisions. For example, we can:

> Provide **choices**,
> Give them a **process** for making decisions,
> **Model** decision making, and
> Use **participatory decision making processes and opportunities** within the family.

Offer choices

We start to teach decision making skills when our child is quite young by giving her choices. Providing choices gives her the skills to weigh alternatives with care, apply the skills of comparing and contrasting, and making final decisions. The choices we give will depend on our child's age and their abilities, or on how much experience they have had with choices. Giving choices allows very young children to make small decisions and it allows older children to make larger ones.

Giving children choices acknowledges and supports their need for autonomy and influence.

The kind of choices we give, and the level of accountability we expect, needs to be appropriate to the age and experience of our child. When we give young children a choice about a relatively major decision and then expect them to be accountable ie stick to that decision, it is often expecting too much of them. For example, how many times have we heard about the child who wanted to learn a musical instrument, and the parent went out and bought the instrument and enrolled the child in a term's worth of music lessons.

After about a month, when the novelty had worn off, the child no longer wanted to go to music lessons or to learn the instrument. The parent feels they have invested a large amount of money and believes that it's not good for their child to pull out. "After all they need to learn about commitment! What sort of a lesson would I be teaching my child if she could pull out of things after such a short time?" So the parent rants and raves about commitment and money etc and demands that the child keeps going to lessons till the end of term.

Expecting commitment to a decision and expecting follow through is all dependent on the age of the child. A five or six year old is usually not capable of this level of commitment. It can't be expected of them. If the parent of a child this age agrees to buying an instrument and paying for lessons they need to understand the child may not want to continue lessons till the end of the term. But if the child were 10 or 11 years of age, the parent could expect the child to persevere once they had made the commitment.

We can start giving our children choices when they are still infants. We can offer them two toys, or two kinds of food. As our child becomes a toddler she is given choices of what clothes to wear, what food to eat, what activities to do, what order to do things eg

'Do you want to listen to this book first and then play with the puzzles or do the puzzles first?'

As our child enters the 'terrific twos' we have a great opportunity help him to develop autonomy, skills, and his sense of influence. It is a stage of development to capitalise on, not moan about and label the 'terrible twos'.

The 'terrific twos' is one of the most exciting stages of development. It is a time when we can see our child begin to reach out for their potential. When they declare 'I can do it myself' we can foster this attitude instead of shooting it down. It is a key time to build their self-empowerment foundations. The choices we can give that are suitable for this age are only bounded by our creativity.

Some examples:

"Would you like to wear this green shirt or this one with birds on it?"
"Would you like a banana sandwich or a tomato sandwich?"
"Would you like to play on the swing or kick the ball?"
"Would you like to put your shoes on first or your hat?"

These may not seem like important decisions but to a young child they are very important opportunities to develop autonomy and self-esteem. They are the kind of decisions that give our child the basic skills to advance to more complex decisions making.

All choices have consequences or effects. Sometimes these effects are positive and pleasant and other times they are negative and unpleasant. And sometimes they are neutral. Making decisions and feeling the effects is how children learn. They learn to weigh up the pros and cons, based on the effects of decisions they have made in the past and based on their knowledge and understanding of the world.

As new parents our young children provide us with many opportunities to practice the Dharma. From the ages of 2 years through to 5 years, children allow us a great opportunity to 'let go' of what we thought was important. We have an opportunity to see the world through their eyes and revel in it.

At this age children are largely unaware of the social boundaries of what to wear in different contexts. They love to wear their favourite clothes out shopping or to Grandma's house. When one of my sons was this age he loved to wear rubber boots and wouldn't take them off to go out. He teamed the boots with baggy shorts, a singlet and a series of necklaces from his mother's drawer. This combination drew many stares and comments in the shopping centre.

The choices we offer a school age child could include; which friends to invite over, which movie to see, which food to buy, what to do on the holidays, bedtime etc. As they grow older and more proficient in making decisions the choices become bigger and the consequences greater.

With this increase in ability they also need to have increased accountability for their decisions. For example, an 8 year old who decides on a fried rice meal in a restaurant cannot change his mind once it arrives, just because they changed their mind. There has to be some level of accountability built into their decision making. Otherwise they will not feel the negative or positive effects of their decision and therefore not learn to weigh up more carefully in the future.

When a child enters the young adult age group ie 13 – 16 years of age, the previous training they have had in decision making will put them in a good position to make beneficial decisions. At this age they are faced with decisions of conformity and fitting in. Peer pressure is particularly strong at this age and if they have had a lot of practice making decisions in the preceding years they will be in a better position to make wise and compassionate decisions. At this age they face the choice to smoke or not; to drink or not; to come home on time or not, etc.

As we observe our young adult making wise decisions we can give them more freedom to set their own limits. For example if we find our son is regularly coming home on, or before, the time agreed upon, we may choose to let him set his own time. We need to know what time this is, but if he is showing that he can make sound choices he is ready to have more say in his life.

What is the decision making process

We can help our child to become self-empowered by providing him with a process for making decisions. The decision making process is similar to the solution focussed approach to problem solving, and follows the following steps:

Define the problem or situation: 'What would you like to be different?' 'What would you like to be the outcome?' 'What are your needs?' 'What are other people's needs?'

Gather information or alternatives: 'What is happening in this situation?' 'Who is involved?' 'What would give you the outcome you would like?' (brainstorm) 'Would this be a positive outcome for other people involved?'

Weigh up the pros and cons of the alternatives: 'What is 'good' or 'bad' about each alternative you have suggested?' 'How will each one affect other people?'

Make a decision: 'Which alternative do you like the most?' 'Which one are you going to go with?'

What will happen if I carry through?: 'If you choose that one what will happen?' 'Are other people involved in this decision?'

Implement the decision: 'Your child takes the action they decided on.'

Evaluate the decision based on effects: 'What happened when you took that action?' 'Did it affect other people?' 'What can you learn from that?' 'Are there any other situations where this also would work?'

We can use this decision making process when our child is faced with making a decision or when they have a problem. We can also help them to learn decision-making and solution-finding skills when we prepare them for unexpected events. It is a good idea to prepare our child for some situations they might encounter eg if he becomes lost in the shopping centre, or if his friend asks him to do something he think is dangerous, or if he is home alone and someone comes to the door.

The more our child practices the decision making process the quicker it will become automatic.

There is an extra bonus to our child making decisions. Decision making stimulates the brain and encourages children's creativity. It encourages our children to think and view the world from a solution focus.

Model decision making for our children

Children learn from how we do things. We provide a very valuable model. If we talk to children about decisions we are making and how we are making these decisions they will see more value in the process. We don't need to involve children in decisions that they are too young to understand or that might worry them, but there are plenty of other decisions we make that we can use to model the process. For example, we may be faced with a change of job – 'will I change or not', we may need to decide what food to cook for a party. Perhaps the decision relates to the purchase of a particular item eg a pot plant. There are so many decisions we make on a daily basis, it is easy to use some to help our child learn how to make decisions.

Participatory decision making process and opportunities

A participatory decision making process involves all family members in being part of decisions that affect the family. We, as parents, often make decisions ourselves because it is easier and quicker, not because it is more appropriate. We can take the time to involve other family members in the decision making process. This not only teaches our children participatory decision making and self-empowerment, it also gives us decisions that family members own. If people own decisions they are more likely to go along with them.

We can involve family members in deciding the weekly menu; whether to invite friends over for dinner; weekend recreation; job sharing around the home; buying a dog; etc. All these decisions affect members of the family and all members need to be involved in the decision making process.

The process we use for participatory family decision making is not much different from decision making with just one other person. What is different is that everyone needs to be heard. Our role is to facilitate the process in such a way that everyone's views are taken into account. This is where our compassionate communication skills come to the fore. When family members disagree we can use empathic listening and respectful expression to bring their needs and feelings to the attention of others.

When we discuss topics where there are differing views and needs within the family it may be necessary to use conflict resolution skills to negotiate a decision. Apparent 'democratic' conflict resolution strategies such as voting, are far from satisfactory as they create winners and losers and the process results in a large minority feeling disempowered. Some useful ways of dissolving a deadlock are 'meet in the middle'; 'go for more'; and 'alternate'.

"*Meet in the middle*" is simply a compromise where everyone bends a little and reaches agreement. "*Go for more*" is a technique where we open the discussion for more ideas. This often brings out more suggestions with a better chance of gaining agreement from everyone. The last option *(alternate)* is to see if everyone will agree to go with one suggestion now and another one next time. For example, if there were two possible recreation activities for the weekend and the family was split between the two, perhaps they would agree to do one this weekend and the other the next weekend.

Many families find it useful to have a set time they meet to make decisions that affect the family. These meetings can be called by any name: family meetings, family conference, family decision time. The name is not important.

Other parents feel they don't need to have specific meetings to make decisions since they feel they make decisions as things come up and need to be decided. Although this is good practice, it can be beneficial to children to know that there are regular meetings where they can bring their own agenda items for the family to help them make decisions, and where they know they will be able to have an input to other decisions. Sometimes a child may be having a difficulty with someone else in the family, or with a friend, and they might want everyone's ideas on a solution.

The meetings don't have to be formal, but an agenda is usually necessary. Sometimes it is also a good idea for someone to write up agreements or outcomes from the meeting. This role can be rotated amongst family members who can write. It is a good idea to rotate the facilitation role too. This provides children with an opportunity to practice a valuable skill that they will need more and more in their lives as they become more involved in school, community and work activities.

Whatever the forum you choose for family decision making, make sure it is fun. Nobody wants to go to a meeting that is either boring or where only negative things are discussed and decided.

Building Resilient Children
and Connected Relationships
with Your Children

Do not do anything harmful;
Do only what is good;
Purify and train your own mind:
This is the teaching of the Buddha;
This is the path to enlightenment.

Buddha

This second last chapter shows us ways to help our children develop resilience and ways for us to develop connected relationships with our children. It shows us which skills and strategies from Buddha Heart Parenting will achieve this and which other activities will add richness and strength to their resilience and to the relationship we share.

The importance of resilience

As parents we want to help our child build resilience. We want them to have an ability to effectively deal with hardship and events in life, which have the potential to cause pain and suffering. Resilience also safeguards our child against becoming involved in activities that may cause them harm, such as drug taking, dangerous driving, and crime.

How do we build resilience in our child?

Many of the skills and strategies that are covered in this book build resilience. These combined with an understanding of Buddhist philosophy will stand our child in good stead when they encounter difficult situations. Both Buddha Heart Parenting and Buddhist principles build resilience and strength in our child.

Our resilient child has:

Self-awareness. Much of our strength is in knowing who we are and knowing our beliefs. The practice of looking deeply, which we encourage through empathic listening and self-expression, allows our child to understand herself. She then has the ability to know her needs and where her feelings and emotions come from. She is able to examine her mind and accept responsibility for what she is thinking and feeling.

Internal locus of control. A resilient child looks inside to determine what is right for them. They are not swayed by friends or by the media, to do something they know is not 'right'. Their self-concept is based on criteria they set not by the value judgements of others.

Decision making & solution finding skills. Resilient children know how to explore alternatives, weigh up pros and cons of possible courses of action or decisions, and are able to make decisions based on compassion and wisdom. They are able to see situations from a broader perspective to determine what is beneficial and what is not. These skills not only give them skills to make decisions and solve problems, they give them the confidence to know that whatever comes their way, they will be able to find a way forward. Having a solution focus means our children are creative and resourceful thinkers.

Compassion and wisdom. The skills and strategies of Buddha Heart Parenting allow our children to develop compassion and empathy for others. When they combine this with the wisdom they gain from understanding and practicing Buddhism, they are resilient.

Autonomy. Buddha Heart Parenting supports children to develop autonomy whilst still making a deep connection to all life around them. When our child has autonomy and feels the interdependence of all things they are able to make decisions and act with the 'good of all' in mind. They are able to withstand pressure to act in ways contrary to Buddhist principles and are able to bounce back from temporary hardship.

Effective communication skills. Effective communication skills support our child to develop and maintain meaningful friendships. When our child can use empathic listening to look deeply into others to understand their feelings and needs, and are able to respectfully express their own feelings and needs, they are valued as a friend. Their relationships are enduring and meaningful. The ability to connect with people in this way provides social support and strengthens resilience in our child.

Opportunities to help others. When our child focuses outwards and seeks to help and support others they develop resilience. Helping others increases their feelings of empowerment and sense of value. They can do this by engaging in age-appropriate volunteer work in the community or we can ask them to help us with tasks we are doing.

An understanding of Buddhist principles. When our child has an understanding of basic Buddhist principles and concepts, they tend to make wise decisions, and they tend to be shielded from possible pain and suffering. When they understand dependent origination they make wise decisions because they understand they are responsible for their thoughts, words and actions, and that all action has effects – both positive and negative. When they understand impermanence they realise that whatever their circumstances are now, they will not last – this applies to both positive and negative circumstances. Change is part of life. When they understand emptiness they understand the oneness of all things and this understanding supports wise decisions. A basic understanding of Buddhism will encourage our child to seek happiness from inside, instead of from the outside world.

Developing connected relationships with our children

Buddha Heart Parenting is all about connecting with our child at a deeper level. The underlying ethos of Buddha Heart Parenting provides the fabric for deep connection. The skills and strategies provide the weave. As our child learns and uses the skills and strategies themselves, the connection will deepen. The skills and strategies outlined in this book will enhance our relationships when we combine them with activities that share joy in living and playing.

Ingredients for connected relationships

Attitude and motivation

If we use Buddha Heart Parenting with an underlying attitude and motivation of compassion and loving-kindness, where we aim to support our child to develop their Buddha potential, we will develop a deep connection to our child. Children pick up our underlying attitudes and motivations more easily than they understand our words. When we combine compassion and wisdom in our parenting we encourage our child to make deep connections not only with us but with others as well.

Compassionate communication

One of the greatest tools for creating and maintaining a deep connection with our child is communication, compassionate communication. Compassionate communication becomes a two-way process as our child becomes more experienced in using the skills. Compassionate communication is based on respect, equality and compassion for both our child and ourself. It allows us, and our child, to share feelings and needs and arrive at beneficial solutions to some of the difficulties of family living and so strengthen our connection.

Treat our child as our best friend

All interactions with our child are based on recognition of their Buddha nature. If we find ourself talking to our child in ways we wouldn't talk to our friend, then we are not connected. When we recognise their Buddha nature all our communication with our child, whether verbal or non-verbal is respectful. Our words are respectful, our tone of voice is respectful, and our body language is respectful. When we talk with our child it is important to stop what we are doing and attend. Really be there. Give eye contact. Show them we respect them and that they are important to us.

> A family is a place where a mind lives with other minds. If these minds love each other the home will be as beautiful as a flower garden.
> The Teachings of Buddha.

Listen to our child

When we listen to our child, really listen, we will find we create a connection that is fulfilling to both of us. Our child will feel we care about him, he will feel respected and feel he has someone he can come to when he needs to.

Have fun with our child

Having fun together can strengthen connections. We can make the time to play with our child more often. We can't build a connected relationship with our child unless we spend time with them. When we play with them, we can really play with them and be mindfully in the moment.

It doesn't matter what we play, just playing, have fun, enjoying it is the key. This makes the time we spend with them really quality time. If we have a really busy schedule it may seem difficult to make the time but what is more important in the long term? Our child matters.

Eat meals together

Eating is a sharing time. It sets the stage for conversation and fun. Mealtime can be one of the most looked-forward to times in the day when the whole family can be together and share food and conversation. This allows us to deepen our connection with our child. It also provides our child with an opportunity to connect with their food. The Slow Food movement is a growing movement worldwide that seeks to bring back a connection to food, traditional recipes (not fast food or pre-prepared meals), and connection to people. Many children don't know how their food is grown or where their food is grown, and some don't know how a meal is made. We can help all these connections to develop and deepen when we eat together.

Create special times

Make time to give each of our children 'special' time. It's important they know this is their time with us and that other members of the family will also have their own 'special' time. Some parents make bedtime a special time for young children. As children grow older we can make a different time if that is more acceptable to them.

Support their self-empowerment

Using the skills and strategies of Buddha Heart Parenting allows our child to become self-empowered. We can take whatever opportunity presents itself to support this process. Children will often feel more empowered when they assist us with a task we are doing.

Set minimum realistic guidelines

Children have a greater sense of belonging when they have boundaries or guidelines that are consistently upheld. As we saw earlier in participatory decision making, if children are a part of setting guidelines they feel valued, included and empowered. This involvement also strengthens the connections within the family. It is best if guidelines are as few as possible and are clear.

Our relationship with our children lasts a lifetime. If we put the work in now we will be able to reap the rewards for a long time.

When we make use of this fortunate position as parents to practice engaged Buddhism we will benefit both as a Buddhist and as a parent. Our children will also benefit through the support we give them to realise their Buddha nature.

Until you reach the path,
You wander the world
With the precious Buddha
Completely wrapped up inside
As in a bundle of rags
..you have this precious Buddha. Unwrap it quickly!
                                                                    Buddha

Have Compassion For Yourself

If you want others to be happy, practice compassion.
If you want to be happy, practice compassion.

Dalai Lama.

This final chapter focuses on making sure we have compassion for ourself in the task we have set. It also provides some tips for how to approach the changes we intend to make.

Buddhism in all its forms needs to be embodied. That is, it needs to be lived. Parenting provides us the perfect vehicle to do this. We can act as Buddha would. We can be a Buddha on a practical level. Even those strands of Buddhism that emphasise meditation, advise us that meditation may begin on the mat, but it ends everywhere. We are instructed to take our meditation into our daily life with the ultimate goal of our entire life becoming a meditation. This is good advice. Little by little we can achieve this.

As we work on being a Buddha and integrating Buddha Heart Parenting into our daily life, we are practising real Buddhism in real life. As we use the skills, we move beyond reading and thinking to really *doing* – really travelling the Buddhist path.

Buddha Heart Parenting is an extremely rewarding way to parent. We will see our child blossom as we learn to use compassion and wisdom in our interactions with them. This frees us both to really have fun together. Life is joyous.

Having read all about Buddha Heart Parenting, you are probably keen to put the skills and strategies into effect.

Remember that patterns of thinking and behaviour can be difficult to change. It may take time and consistent effort before we give up our old inappropriate ways of doing things.

If we set ourself realistic goals and put in consistent effort we will succeed. The single most effective thing we can do is to change the way we think. When we change the way we view the world and all that happens in it, we will automatically drop some of our inappropriate reactions to our children and their behaviour.

By learning the skills and strategies of Buddha Heart Parenting and applying them to our parenting, we will be working to support the changes we are making in how we view the world. The two approaches work hand in hand and make us doubly effective.

Many parents become discouraged when they don't progress as fast as they want. We can set realistic goals. If we fall back into old patterns, we can accept that this will happen sometimes, especially in the early stages, and just move on. We will make it.

When we first change the way we talk to our children or how we respond to their inappropriate behaviour, our children may appear to increase their inappropriate behaviour. They do this because they are used to the way we were reacting to them. They will keep up their inappropriate behaviour in the hope that we will return to our old inappropriate ways of reacting to them. Remember the example I gave of my children who would look in the return slot of public phones? Just as my children took some time to extinguish this behaviour, your children may take time to give up their old way of behaving. The more consistent we are the quicker they will give it up.

Consistency is important. We are more likely to be consistent if we do not try to change too many things at one time. We can set realistic goals for ourself. When we start, we choose only one or maybe two skills to learn and practice. As we master these we can move on to learn more. As we work on our inner development, learning the skills of Buddha Heart

Parenting will become easier because there will be internal and external alignment.

One of the biggest hurdles we face is in eradicating attachment and aversion. If we work on getting rid of these we will not give ourself such a hard time for slipping back into old ways. We can learn to let go of things. We can realise that what is possible, is possible and nothing more.

In the early stages before we have developed sufficient skills and strategies we may find it useful to have some mantras or affirmations that keep us focused. The following affirmations may be helpful. We can put them on the bathroom mirror, on the fridge, on the back of the toilet door.

> *"This (our child's inappropriate behaviour) is just for attention."*
> *"I am working on developing a good relationship, I will not allow this behaviour to distract me from that."*
> *"It is the long term change that is important."*
> *"All things are impermanent, this situation included."*

From my experience with thousands of parents, I know that when parents put consistent effort into developing their Buddha heart and changing their parenting approach to that of Buddha Heart Parenting, transformation does occur.

The single most important thing we can do in life is to develop our Buddha heart.
The second most important thing is to parent our children from our Buddha heart.

May all merit generated by
the creation and reading of
this book benefit all sentient beings
without partiality.

Words to build
your Feeling Vocabulary

abandoned
abused
accepted
afraid
alarmed
alienated
alone
aloof
amazed
amused
anger
angst
anguish
annoyed
antagonized
anxious
apathetic
appalled
appreciated
apprehensive
ashamed
astonished
astounded
attacked
belittled
bereft
betrayed
bewildered
bitterness
bored
bothered
bullied
burdened
calm

cantankerous
cautious
challenged
cheerful
comforted
committed
compassion
competitive
compliant
composed
concern
condescending
confident
confused
connected
contempt
contentment
contrary
controlled
courageous
criticized
cross
crushed
cynical
daunted
defeat
defective
defensive
defiant
degraded
dejected
delight
demeaned
dependent

depressed
deprived
despair
detached
determined
devastated
disagreeable
disappointed
disconcerted
disconnected
discouraged
disgraced
disgust
dishearten
disillusioned
disinterested
disliked
dismay
disorganized
dissatisfied
distracted
distraught
distress
disturbed
dominated
ecstatic
edgy
elated
embarrassed
emotional
empathetic
empowered
encouraged
engrossed

enraged
enraptured
enthusiastic
envious
exasperation
excited
exhausted
exhilaration
exposed
fatigued
fearful
fearless
foolish
forgiven
forgiving
fretful
friendly
frightened
frustrated
fulfilled
furious
gladness
gleeful
glum
grateful
grief
grieved
grumpy
guilty
happiness
hate
hateful
hatred
heartache

heartbroken	mortified	rejected	testy
hopeful	mournful	rejuvenated	thankful
hopeless	moved	relaxed	threatened
hopelessness	nervous	release	thrilled
horrified	nurturing	relief	tormented
humble	obsessed	reluctant	tortured
humiliated	obstinate	remorse	touched
hurt	offended	repressed	touchy
immobilized	optimistic	repugnant	trusting
impatient	overjoyed	repulsive	turned off
inadequate	overwhelmed	resentful	unafraid
indecisive	pain	reserved	uncaring
indifferent	pained	resigned	unconcerned
indignant	panic	resolute	undeserving
injured	panicked	respected	uneasiness
insecure	passionate	responsible	unfeeling
inspired	patronized	responsive	unhappy
insulted	peaceful	restless	unimportant
irate	peeved	revengeful	uninterested
irritable	pensive	rotten	unmoved
irritated	perplexed	sabotaged	unnerved
isolated	pessimistic	sad	unsettled
jealous	petrified	safe	unsympathetic
jolly	playful	satisfied	upset
joyful	pleased	scared	uptight
jubilant	powerless	scorn	used
judged	preoccupied	secretive	useless
liberated	pressured	secure	vengeful
listless	pride	seductive	victimized
lively	privileged	self-assured	vindicated
livid	protective	shaken	virtuous
loathing	proud	shame	vulnerable
loneliness	provoked	sheepish	warm
lonely	punished	shocked	watchful
longing	put out	silly	weepy
loss	puzzled	skeptical	wimpy
lost	rage	sorrow	withdrawn
loved	rapture	sorry	worked up
loveless	rapturous	spiteful	worried
loving	reassured	stressed	worthless
miserable	rebellious	stupefied	worthy
misunderstood	receptive	sulky	wounded
mixed-up	reckless	sympathy	wretched
moody	reclusive	tearful	wronged
morbid	refreshed	tender	
morose	regret	terror	